Focus on Retirement

Focus on Retirement

Fred Kemp and Bernard Buttle

Kogan Page

First published 1979
by Kogan Page Limited
120 Pentonville Road, London N1

Reprinted in 1979

Copyright © by Fred Kemp and Bernard Buttle

All rights reserved

Printed in Great Britain by
The Anchor Press Ltd, Tiptree, Essex

ISBN 0 85038 183 5
ISBN 0 85038 195 9

Contents

Introduction

We have written this book in the hope that it will be of direct use to people approaching retirement, to those already retired, and to employers and union officials who recognise they have a moral responsibility to ensure that employees nearing retirement have an opportunity to receive advice and guidance in preparing for the next major and indeed critical phase of their lives.

During our years as Director and General Secretary respectively of the Pre-Retirement Association we spoke and listened to hundreds of people who were either facing the prospect of retirement or had recently retired. This close involvement with them demonstrated to us that for many, the sudden change from full-time employment to full-time retirement can be a traumatic experience. We also became convinced that serious thought and sensible preparation for the new way of life ahead can help all those affected to anticipate and so to avoid most of the difficulties which can arise at that time. Forethought and preparation are the cornerstones for making retirement one of the most enjoyable and satisfying periods of one's life.

In the following pages we have made the fullest use of past research and observation in helping us to advise on the problems likely to arise. Experience shows that the fears and worries that beset most people as retirement approaches are usually capable of solution given adequate thought beforehand. Perhaps even more important we have also tried to highlight some of the many opportunities open to people as they enter retirement.

In focusing the reader's attention upon possible problems on the one hand and opportunities on the other, we have been particularly conscious of the fact that we have no special mandate or gift which entitles us to *tell* people what to do (a fact all too often forgotten by some self-styled experts). We appreciate that if you, the reader, are nearing retirement age you have a personal wealth of experience behind you. You are unique — your own character and personal interests are probably very different from those of your neighbours and certainly from ours. One man's meat is another man's poison, but if some of our ideas seem a bit 'toxic' to you we nevertheless hope that you will find enough meat in the rest to sustain you! Once you have accepted that there is a need to plan and prepare for the years ahead, the battle is half won.

Chapters one to nine are primarily directed towards people who are nearing retirement age or who have recently B retired.

The remaining chapters are focused upon the responsibilities of the government, the employers, the trade unions and the voluntary services in developing and providing facilities for retirement training and support services for elderly people in the community. This section of the book also includes a summary of the resource material at present available for retirement education in the form of specialist publications and audio-visual programmes; examples of various types of advisory courses; and a chapter on developments in other countries. This is followed by a schedule of useful addresses of organisations referred to in the preceding chapters.

Perhaps some of our readers, who have found the first part of the book useful to them personally because they are nearing retirement, are still holding positions of authority and influence in their employing organisations. If so, we hope that the second part of our book will demonstrate to them how they might initiate pre-retirement training for colleagues and other employees, or perhaps improve the present provision within their own organisations.

F O Kemp, B W Buttle

Acknowledgements

In writing this book we have been encouraged by the readiness of so many people and organisations to help with information and advice. We wish to record our special thanks and appreciation to:

Back Pain Association

Ivan Brown, writer and lecturer

Dr Don Clarke, Director of the British Life Assurance Trust for Health Education

Edward Eves, author of *Money and Your Retirement*

J Maitland Cook, Director, the Retirement Homes Association

The Health Education Council

Professor Alastair Heron, Chairman and founder Vice-President of the Pre-Retirement Association

David Hobman, Director of Age Concern (England)

Fielden Hughes, author, lecturer and broadcaster

David James, Director of Adult Education, University of Surrey

John Kemp, Managing Director of *Choice* magazine

Ann Kimber, Pre-Retirement Association Information Officer

Morley College, London

Del Pasterfield, Supervisor, Welfare and Benefits Employee Programmes, Ford Motor Company Limited

The Pre-Retirement Association

Spencer & Kent, Chartered Surveyors and Estate Agents

Ron Taylor, Head of Welfare Services, W H Smith
& Son Ltd

G Watkin Williams, former Director, The Retirement
Advisory Bureau, The Institute of Directors

Dr H Beric Wright, President of the Pre-Retirement
Association, Deputy Chairman, BUPA Medical Centre
and Hon Medical Adviser, The Institute of Directors

Chapter 1
In Perspective

Joining the ranks

During the first weeks of retirement, many people suffer a
sense of deprivation. They are cut off from a deeply
established way of life; the familiar daily round which for
decades brought them purpose, discipline and routine. Work
also brought them companionship with others, whether they
were colleagues, clients, customers, or fellow commuters.
We are social beings, and we miss the framework which
work provides.

Retirement is essentially an intensely individual and
personal experience. People react to it in very different ways,
depending upon their mental attitudes and personal
philosophy of life. They have only one thing in common —
their age group. In extreme cases the sense of deprivation can
strike suddenly, as a person leaves for home after the last day
at work. Others start their retirement with a feeling of happy
release. Still others, after those first few days of relaxation,
rush into a frenzy of activity — spring-cleaning, redecorating,
gardening — all of which are intended, perhaps subconsciously,
to fill the gap left when there is no longer the routine of work
to occupy their thoughts and time. This spate of activity may
not last very long, but it does give a breathing space for
settling down and finding new interests. Not least, people's
reactions to retirement will be conditioned by the extent to
which they have prepared for it beforehand.

To all those suffering from a sense of isolation — the
feeling that they have been pushed out of the mainstream
into a forgotten backwater — we say,'Remember that in
reality you are joining the ranks of a great army of people
who have already retired'. No less than 16 per cent of the
population of the United Kingdom are over state retirement

age — that is, men who have reached 65 years of age and women of 60 years or more. The Government Statistical Service in 1976 published figures which show that by 1981 an estimated 9.8 million people will be over state retirement age: ie one person in six! No figures are available to show how this huge number would be still further increased if early retirement were also taken into account. Undoubtedly the increase would be considerable, bearing in mind the tendency in recent years for employers to offer attractive financial incentives to induce staff to accept early retirement. Where over-manning is a problem, early retirement is often introduced in consultation with the unions as an acceptable means of achieving a reduction in the size of the workforce. Apart from early retirements, many unemployed men and women are nearing retirement age. In areas such as Merseyside, they have little chance of further employment. This hidden army is also ignored in the retirement statistics.

Talk of nearly 10 million retired people in the UK may seem a meaningless statistic to some. Perhaps we can illustrate the magnitude involved by making use of other government statistics. The combined populations of Scotland, Wales and Northern Ireland, at nine and a half million, are less than the number of people over state retirement age in the United Kingdom. The population of Greater London is even less, at seven and a half million.

Government statistics			Total population (millions)
People over state retirement age in the UK (1975 mid-year estimates)			9.6
Populations (1976)	(Scotland	5.2)	
	(Wales	2.8)	
	(Northern Ireland	1.5)	9.5
Populations (1976)	Greater London		7.5

What conclusions can be drawn from these statistics?

First, to the newly-retired who feel cut off from former friends and colleagues — remember that your situation is by no means unique! On the contrary, there are another 10 million or so people sharing the same experience. Almost certainly there are several men and women living quite near to you who have also retired from work. You may already be on nodding terms with some of them. Why not put traditional British reserve firmly in its place, and cultivate new friendships?

Secondly, the sheer scale in terms of population involved must surely make retirement a significant factor in any government economic and social strategy. There is continual pressure on government Ministers to improve the lot of the pensioner, whether through increased rates of benefit or through additional facilities to be provided by the health and social services.

The years ahead

There is yet another set of statistics which help to put retirement into perspective. These are concerned with expectation of life. The life expectation of an infant born in the Middle Ages must have been short indeed. Wars, marauding bands of robbers and outlaws, frequent disease, shortage of food and rough shelter, were hazards of the times. No wonder that those who managed to survive were often accorded special privileges in their role as elders, who could be looked to for guidance and counsel drawn from their long experience of life and their accumulated wisdom. Strangely, the modern industrialised society in which we live has not only created the phenomenon of 'retirement' as we know it today, but it no longer credits the older generation with any special attributes. There is, instead, an ever increasing tendency on the part of many employers to appoint younger men and women to senior posts. The argument is that the education and training of younger people is in step with the accelerating pace of modern technology, and furthermore, that the younger executives have the ability and flexibility needed to adapt more readily to new techniques and methodology.

In 1651, Thomas Hobbes declared that life was nasty, brutish and short. Had we lived in his day, we would probably have agreed with him. Nearer our own time, the squalor and social upheaval which resulted from the Industrial Revolution reduced the life expectation of working people.

At the present time, advances in human knowledge, particularly in the fields of medical and scientific research and technology, have enabled statisticians to announce that the life expectancy of a baby born in the United Kingdom today is 69.2 years for a male and 75.5 for a female. (So much for sex equality!)

What people often fail to appreciate is that these statistics — 69.2 and 75.5 years — are valid for a child at *birth*, but do not remain constant. Life statistics in fact show that as children survive those childhood illnesses; as youth learns to avoid its self-made hazards of sport and adventure; and as men and women survive the dangers to health associated with middle age, their life expectancy at birth is steadily extended. This is illustrated by the following life expectation statistics, taken from the *Annual Abstract of Statistics 1977* issued by the Department of Population Census Surveys:

Expectation of life 1973-75

Age	Male	Female
At birth	69.2	75.5
60	15.6	20.2
65	12.3	16.3
70	9.6	12.8
75	7.4	9.7
80	5.7	7.2

We were taken aback when one young trainee personnel manager bounced up at a conference on pre-retirement training to ask whether there was really much point in it all, if the life expectancy for a man retiring at 65 was only another three or four years. Was it cost-effective to spend his company's money for such little return?! To him, 65 years of age seemed an immeasurable distance of time away. He had completely failed to appreciate that there is a progression in life expectancy, as the table indicates. He had to be told, gently, that a man of 65 can reasonably expect to live until he is 77 and a woman of that age even longer, to 81 years. Of course, we are dealing in averages. None of us can predict when our end will come. One cynic suggested that only a statistician dies on time!

The long-term view

If you look at retirement from this perspective, it becomes clear that when people retire they should be concerned not only with the short term — it is not merely a question of relaxing over a long holiday, or having time at last to indulge in a frenzy of 'do-it-yourself', and to put the garden in good order. No — potential pensioners must also try to look ahead in terms of 10/15/20 years. They must take the long-term view.

If you are close to retirement age, think back for a moment over the past 15 to 20 years of your life. Can you recall all the things which have happened in that time — all the changes, the important landmarks, the disappointments and the achievements of those years? It may prove to be quite a test of your memory. So much living is crowded into such a long time.

Now, reverse the process and think how much you might be able to achieve in the next 10 to 15 years. What might you see in your crystal ball? It would certainly have been a barren time if that glimpse into the future showed that you had just sat back in your retirement and let the rest of the world go by.

Perhaps you might try another exercise: imagine yourself at 80 years of age looking back over all the achievements and satisfactions of your life since you retired all those years ago. How sad if that were a retrospect of wasted years!

Whichever way you look at it, you know it makes good sense to carry out some long-term planning and to make careful preparation for the years ahead, which, as we all hope, may be a time of happiness and self-fulfilment — the best time, indeed.

Most of us conformed to the usual pattern of education. We spent the first few years of life with our mothers, learning to walk and talk, absorbing the ways of life around us and discovering new wonders each day. The next 10 to 15 years or so were spent in full-time education. Much of it was intended to prepare us to play a useful part in the work-orientated society in which we live. The learning process continued after we had embarked on our working career. Whatever job we took when we left school, college, or university, we still had to be trained — we still had to study and learn. Even when we grew more mature and progressed up the promotion ladder, we were still expected to keep abreast of new developments by attending training courses, participating in refresher courses, and conferences; and perhaps by reading technical papers and professional journals.

When we have to spend so much of that first 'growing-up' phase of our lives preparing for the second phase — our working lives — is it reasonable to expect to leap from that second phase into the third major phase of our lives — retirement — without any preparation whatsoever? A person's working life and the preparation for it may seem to be of paramount importance to the young and the middle-aged. That, after all, is the extent of their personal experience. It is difficult for them to spare much time for thoughts of retirement. It has no place in their experience, and so has little relevance in their scheme of things. Thoughts of retirement are pushed aside to be dealt with when that distant day arrives. They are complacent and feel, smugly, that by the time they reach retirement age, their knowledge and experience of life will enable them to get by in one way or another. Our message to all those approaching retirement with rather vague, unformed ideas, or seeing the leisured future through rose-tinted spectacles, is that it is well worthwhile clearing the vision and taking a long cool look at what the future might hold. It will help to get retirement into proper perspective. We hope that we can assist you to *focus on retirement.*

Points to remember

1. Retirement is an intensely individual experience, but paradoxically, you are joining a multitude of other people who have also retired. You are *not* alone.
2. Statistics show that for the vast majority, retirement is not just a matter of months, but of many years ahead.
3. People who take the trouble to plan and prepare for their retirement rather than just letting it happen are far more likely to find it enjoyable and self-fulfilling.

Chapter 2

TheVital Adjustment

What do we mean by adjustment?

Whatever our circumstances in life, most of our daily routines, surroundings, and the events which occupy our minds, are familiar to us. Nothing is ideal, but we have learned to get used to things; there is comfort in the familiar. When change comes, we do not always like it; most of us resist change for change's sake. Even changes we look forward to, and which we know will be of benefit to us, often unsettle us to begin with. Young people look forward to growing up, to being allowed to act as adults; there is the excitement of going to college or university; the thrill of living away from home for the first time; the new job; marriage; becoming a parent — all these experiences can be worthwhile, but they often bring stresses and strains as we adjust to new circumstances and relationships. The time of greatest strain and uncertainty can occur at the changeover from full-time work to retirement — a transition from one way of life to another. If we recognise that a fundamental change is taking place and that adjustments have to be made, we can try to prepare ourselves and our attitude to what is inevitable. Changes in the pattern of our life involve adjustments, and the adjustment required of us at retirement is a vital one.

In preparing for the adjustment to retirement, let us take stock of what we shall need in our new life-style.

Criteria for a successful retirement

Professor Alastair Heron, founder Vice-President, and now Chairman of the Pre-Retirement Association, suggested in the early PRA booklet *Solving New Problems*, that there are six basic needs for a happy retirement:

1. Good physical and emotional health.
2. Adequate income, substantially above subsistence level.
3. Suitable accommodation.
4. Congenial associates and neighbours.
5. One or more absorbing interests.
6. An adequate personal philosophy of life.

The first item in Professor Heron's list is good physical and emotional health. The state of our health may set limits to what we can do, but whatever our state of health we can still do as much as we are capable of. There are many who have triumphed over severe disabilities, because they put the emphasis on what they could do, rather than trying for perfect health before starting anything!

Each of the first five needs in the list is the subject of a separate chapter in this book, and each is an important ingredient in the recipe for a successful retirement. Yet it would be an over-simplification to suggest that people facing the complete change in their way of life that retirement brings will be absolutely all right if they look after their health, sort out their finances, keep themselves occupied, find new friends, and develop new interests. If we think about Professor Heron's list again, we see that these requirements will vary from person to person. What is 'adequate' or 'suitable' for one person will not necessarily be so for another. The first five items in the list can be measured, in the sense that we can check to see if we have enough of them.

Item six is of a different kind; how can we be sure that we have a personal philosophy of life which is suitable for us personally? Yet in some ways, item six is the most important in the list. If this one is right, we can put up with deficiencies in any of the others. But if number six is out of tune, the lack of harmony may make us discontented with what could otherwise be a good enough level in the other five. We all know someone who appears to be comfortably off and yet is full of troubles and worries, and whose main topic of conversation is about things that have gone wrong, or fears of what may go wrong.

This chapter is concerned with questions of adjustment, and with the sixth need in the list. People's attitudes to retirement; their acceptance of the need for adjustments in their way of thinking; a personal view of what life is all about — all these are fundamental and form a thread which should be running through discussions of all the other needs listed.

The sixth need is concerned with matters of personal belief about life — about man's place in the cosmos, and about what makes living a meaningful condition. At a Symposium on Preparation for Retirement held in Oslo in November 1977, Professor Heron presented a paper in which he drew attention to some of the crucial problems. He pointed out that, 'during the lifetimes of those now moving towards retirement a great many of the values, and of the social attitudes based upon those values, have changed and changed radically . . . There are very few certainties available to most adults today.' He believed that many difficulties were due to the inadequacies of the educational processes through which the vast majority of people have passed. Education should be a life-long process, and in the long term, pre-retirement education would become unnecessary if there were to be 'a very substantial change in the nature, the content, the timing and the provision of education throughout the lifespan of each individual'. There should be 'some form of recurrent educational provision as a legal right of the individual to be taken up at various times from childhood to old age'.

It is true that most people are so immersed in the everyday hustle and bustle of their working lives that they have little time to think of the deeper issues of life. But well before the time for retirement looms, people need to take stock of themselves; to think about personal relationships with family and friends (as we discuss in the next chapter); and to consider how to make retirement a rewarding experience and an exciting new phase of their lives.

Accepting the need for adjustment

This is of course the first essential step — a willingness to accept that retirement will arrive and that it will mean fundamental changes. Imagine a senior executive, soon to retire, arriving at his office with the customary bulging briefcase. He is firmly convinced that the place will come to a grinding halt when he has to leave — in fact they will *have* to keep him on! He may possibly agree that preparation for retirement is a good idea — for other people, but not for him. Sadly, our senior executive cannot accept that he is not indispensable. Like many men and women holding down important and demanding jobs, he is not prepared to think about retirement. He is rather like the small child who thinks, 'If I shut my eyes, maybe the tiger will go away.' So he erects an imaginary brick wall just high enough to prevent his looking over the top and seeing what awaits him on the other side.

Executives and managers are often the people most at risk on retirement. Their jobs have meant so much to them, for so long, that they have had no time for other interests. For some, even the occasional game of golf or other social event is undertaken only because it is in the interests of the job. For these 'dedicated' men and women, retirement could mean boredom, frustration and general misery for themselves and those around them. They suffer a sense of bereavement — job bereavement. It is ironic that the very people unwilling to acknowledge that they should face up to the need to prepare and plan for their retirement are those who, in their jobs, would think it the height of folly to promote a new scheme or product without exhaustive preliminary research, testing, marketing surveys and financial appraisals so as to assess viability and chances of success.

This unwillingness to come to terms with retirement was forcibly illustrated to us by a 61-year-old former executive who lived quite near the Pre-Retirement Association office. He called one day to offer his services. Anything would do — making the tea, doing the post, filing — anything which would make him feel useful. He had retired six months previously from a senior appointment where, as he said, 'I was accustomed to making important and far-reaching decisions every day. Yet today, the biggest decision I have to make is whether to have sausages or a chop for lunch.' He joked about his frustration, but it was apparent that under the surface he was miserable and unhappy. He had been unable to come to terms with retirement. Fortunately, we were able to help him adopt a more positive approach and through discussion, we encouraged him to develop his latent interest in journalism which, in time, gave him a new sense of purpose.

When it comes to retirement, the more fortunate are likely

to be those who do a job which they can easily put out of their minds as they leave their office, factory or shop after the day's work. These are the people who have had the time and opportunity over the years to build up other interests and activities which have nothing to do with their work. For them, retirement means greater opportunity to develop these interests and expand their hobbies and activities still further. Yet they too have to accept the need for adjustments in their way of thinking, to take stock, and to review relationships with those about them. But we should not over-emphasise the difficulties for executives and managers — by and large they usually have more material, educational and cultural resources to call upon, once they have seen the need for fundamental adjustments.

In 1976, the Division of Social Affairs, United Nations Office in Geneva, produced a paper on preparation for retirement under the European Social Development Programme. This extract is relevant to this problem of adjustment:

'The person who during active life has identified himself too much with his work may easily find himself at a loss on retirement. This feeling may be reinforced by the attitudes of others, used to seeing or taking into consideration mainly the functions of people. Yet, more often than not, retirement is the moment when one can suddenly count only on one's personal value. In the light of this, it would seem that one should start one's apprenticeship for retirement well before the crucial moment comes. It can often be observed that, while the lowering of the retirement age may be vindicated, people become anxious and afraid when it eventually approaches. One of the consequences of this, which might seem paradoxical but is explainable psychologically, is that one hesitates to face and to pepare for it.'

F Le Gros Clark and F S Milligan, in another early PRA booklet, *The Years Still Unexplored* wrote:

'When men first leave their ordinary employment for good and all, they have ideas and plans that are as varied as human nature itself. But one thing is clear. We have to be prepared to draw at last upon all our reserves of personal philosophy. Once work has left you and with it the regular routine of a working day, you have to fall back more and more upon your own inner resources.'

Our attitudes are generally formed from the accumulated experience of our lives, the environment we live in, and the influences of family and the working and social groups with which we associate. Retirement is a new experience, which cuts us off from the working environment and our workaday associates. Our attitudes are inevitably influenced and adjusted to meet the new situation. How successful we are will depend upon our personal philosophy of life. This in itself might be influenced and perhaps strengthened by the new experience of retirement, by continued learning, and by seeking the guidance of others whose opinions we respect, and who appear to have found satisfaction and fulfilment in their lives.

The philosopher Nietzsche wrote, 'He who has a *why* to live can bear with almost any *how*'. In other words, although we cannot control all that happens to us (and cannot always command sufficient of the first three needs listed by Professor Heron) we can begin to control our reaction to what happens, and our response. We can try and feel responsible for the way we live our own life.

The positive approach

It is important also to emphasise that preparation for retirement is not just a matter of learning how to foster and maintain our dwindling resources during our twilight years, nor merely of finding pleasant ways of filling the empty hours while we await the inevitable end. Preparation for retirement and the value of retirement planning is not just a question of preparation and planning for old age! Clearly it is wise to look at some aspects of retirement more than others in the long term — for example in the chapter on living arrnagements we suggest that before sinking your capital into buying a bungalow with a few acres of ground in the depths of the country, you should look ahead 10 or 15 years. You may realise that by then that large garden might have become an unmanageable problem rather than a pleasure, and the lack of public transport, shops and medical facilities could cause difficulties. No — we should recognise that our development is a life-long process; that the adjustments that we have to make in our search for a new sense of purpose in life require a positive approach and not a passive surrender to future dependence and old age.

Not only the money

Retirement means a separation from a life-time's work, normally spanning some 40 years. This long and valuable experience of our working lives should help us to discover what our needs are likely to be in retirement. We can draw upon our own experience to help us meet the challenge of a fundamentally new way of life — to recognise and to make the adjustments in our attitudes and relationships with others which will give us hope and confidence in this new phase.

Drawing on past experience is no new method. A barrister would never dream of giving a formal opinion on a point of law without first seeking precedents in reports of similar cases already decided by the Courts.

Many senior executives and managers are high on the list of 'workaholics' — people who live for their work to the exclusion of nearly everything else in life. It is easy to see that these 'workaholics' get far more out of their jobs than the material benefits made available by the money they earn! The truth is, that no matter how much or how little we enjoy our work, it means a lot more to us than the monthly salary cheque or the weekly pay packet. For most men and women nearing retirement, their lives have revolved around their job for a good many years. Even if they look on work as a necessary evil, endured because it is the only way open to them of making a reasonable livelihood, it still forms a very significant part of their lives, if only for the time and energy they have to devote to it each day. Some of them even use most of their *spare* time in grumbling about their job and everything associated with it!

Of course we work in order to earn money. For many people nearing retirement, the most worrying problem is how they will ever be able to manage financially when they have collected their last salary cheque, and their pension is their only source of income. Perhaps the following chapter on money matters will help to ease minds on that score.

What else, then, do we get from work besides the money? Let us consider the main items in turn.

1. A PURPOSE AND OBJECTIVE
No organisation could survive for long if it employed people to do work which had no definite purpose. Even the least

inquisitive among us would hardly go on working, day in and day out, without knowing or finding out the purpose of our job. Whether our job is personnel manager in British Steel, quality control supervisor for Fords, fashion buyer for Debenhams, typing pool supervisor for IBM, or digging holes in the road for the County Council, we all know (despite some of those old jokes) the purpose of our work.

What then of retirement? Suddenly we are, ourselves, in sole charge of our destinies. We are the boss. We can, for the first time, do what we want with our time — and we will have plenty of that and to spare. If we are not to succumb to apathy; if we are not to make our retirement years merely our 'cabbage' years, we need to discover a new sense of purpose in our lives and to set new personal objectives. We still need our targets and our organisational goals. Too many people enter into retirement rather like a rudderless ship, drifting this way or that, depending upon the vagaries of wind and tide. When you retire you become the captain. *You* set the course and *your* hand is on the tiller. In many ways, work wraps us in a safe cocoon which protects us from having to think about wider issues. In this sense, retirement brings us a greater personal responsibility — we have to consider our purpose in life and must determine our *own* course for *ourselves.*

We have a new freedom *from* restraint and constrictions, but can we use that freedom *for* living our lives? Self-discipline and self-direction is necessary. We need to build up something to replace the support of the daily work routine and colleagues.

2. STATUS AND IDENTITY

Your job also gives you a status in society — a sense of identity. When you meet someone for the first time, even if it happens to be just a casual meeting at the club, in the train, or at a social gathering, it is a safe bet that the question will soon arise — 'What line of business are you in?' or, more directly, 'What's your job, then?' If you are being formally introduced, you are usually given a label to go with your name: 'Meet John — he's with the Midland Bank Trustee Department, you know.' or: 'This is Jane — she's the district nurse.'

Whatever your job is, it carries with it a status and identity for you, and unless you happen to work for MI5 your occupation forms a ready-made starting point for conversation. When asked about your work you are on familiar ground, and can happily talk about it for as long as you can hold the interest of your listener.

Things are changed when you retire. There is still a possibility that your old label will stick, for a time: 'Meet John — he *used* to be an executive with the bank, you know.' or: 'This is Jane — she *used* to be a district nurse.' Somehow it isn't the same. You are far more likely to be labelled just 'retired', for no one is what he 'used to be'. He is what he is . . . now!

Many retired folk, who have not yet discovered a new sense of purpose in their lives, exist in the past to such an extent that their main topic of conversation is about the job they *used* to do. It goes something like this: 'Yes, I can remember when . . .' or 'In my time we had to . . .' or even, 'So I told the Chief . . . and he said . . . so I said . . .' and so on.

The listener usually tries to show a polite interest, but the same old theme quickly becomes boring, especially if the listener cannot get a word in edgeways. There is then the danger that 'bore' will become the operative word. Yet we must not decry the habit of old friends and colleagues recalling memories and chewing over the past. There is nothing wrong in this, and reminiscing can be a pleasant pastime when chatting with others who have the time and the same inclination.

In our experience, the majority of people who are happily making a success of their retirement are those who have carved out and created a new identity for themselves since they retired. For them the label may have changed to: 'Meet John — he's on the Council, and Chairman of the Bowling Club.' Or, 'This is Jane — she is one of the leading lights at our community centre, and runs the local Red Cross.' Maybe neither of these roles appeals to you, but as you read on we may yet strike the right chord for you, or at least help you to find the right notes!

3. SOCIAL CONTACTS AND GROUP SUPPORT
The Working Party on Preparation for Retirement set up by the Social Affairs Committee of the Council of Europe, issued its report in 1977. At one point it stated that one of the

major difficulties for a retired person in an industrialised
society is the loss of the role of an active worker or employee,
a loss which is threefold:

— loss of contact with fellow workers
— loss of the sense of security gained as a member of the
  work group
— a radical change in the rhythm of life

There must be only a very small number of people whose
work is so solitary that they have little or no contact with
fellow workers. Most people find the opportunity, during
their working day, to chat about such mundane things as the
weather, the rush hour, what happened yesterday evening or
over the weekend, the new series on television, the latest
headline news in the morning paper, and so on. Whatever it
is that you chat about with your colleagues, even if it is
having a grumble about the job, and even if you don't
particularly like the people you work with, your job does
provide you with social contacts. Your work presents you,
willy-nilly, with a whole series of personal relationships —
maybe with fellow-commuters, customers or clients, in
addition to your own colleagues and fellow workers. You
have a ready-made outlet for your day-to-day news and a
sounding board for your opinions and views.

Similarly, work gives you a sense of security. You are one
of a team, working towards a common objective. Your
colleagues are there, on the spot, willing to listen to your
troubles. They are people to whom you can readily turn for
advice and support.

Retirement cuts you off from this ready-made audience.
Your circle is suddenly drastically reduced. Yet humans are
gregarious beings. Unlike the tiger, they do not seek to walk
alone in their solitude. We all need those social contacts —
contacts which we tended to take for granted at work.
Human beings *need* to feel secure, to belong, to have self-
respect and the recognition of others. When the working life
comes to an end we have to look to our personal
relationships with family and friends to satisfy all these needs.

Retirement should be looked on as providing an opportunity
for making new friends and renewing old friendships. A retired
person who, through circumstances, has to live alone, runs the
risk of becoming a 'four-walled' person, someone who has

failed to get out of the house and make the effort to create new personal relationships. For many people, as they begin to find a new sense of purpose, as they seek to create a new identity for themselves rather than accepting the passive role of a retired person, new relationships and social contacts come automatically. These relationships and contacts are likely to be more satisfying because they are made with others having like interests.

4. ROUTINE AND DISCIPLINE
In a sense, the daily routine of our working lives is in itself a discipline. Over the years we become thoroughly used to the discipline of the alarm clock, breakfast, travelling to work, getting there at the appointed hour, lunch, and finally packing up for the day and travelling home.

Take, for instance, Alec Watson, who had been a long-serving Local Government officer. He and his wife lived near the Town Hall. For years he had arrived at his office at 9.00 am, home for lunch at 1.00 pm, back at 2.15 pm, and finish at 5.00 pm. On retirement, Alec and his wife were glad to relax the old routine. In the winter they would rise later, have a mid-morning breakfast and maybe miss lunch. Then perhaps a cold snack in the afternoon and a late evening meal before watching the late-night film on television. They had no one else to worry about, and could choose their own times. Unfortunately, after some weeks of the new style of living, the discipline of the years tried to reassert itself. Poor Mr Watson's stomach began to rebel — it never knew what to expect next, or when! He grew steadily more miserable and unwell until, luckily, a friend happened to spot the cause and prescribed an effective remedy — back to a regular routine.

People engaged in other spheres of work may have very different hours of work from the nine to five routine. Nevertheless, for all of us there is some established routine, whatever its pattern, until retirement. So when the discipline and framework of the job is no longer there, it is wise to cultivate a measure of self-discipline. Some retired people find this difficult unless they can inject some other regular commitment into their routine.

Recently, we talked to two retired people who each spent one day a week at the local hospital as voluntary helpers. They both felt that apart from the tremendous satisfaction they found in doing something worthwhile and helping others, their new-found voluntary work brought a valuable measure of self-discipline into their lives. As Mr Long said: 'I know that on one day a week at least, I have to get up early, get washed and shaved, put on a collar and tie, and make myself reasonably presentable for my day at the hospital — it keeps me up to the mark.' Mrs White fully agreed with him, apart from the shaving and collar and tie bit! They both felt needed again. They realised that the patients depended on their visits.

In time, retirement brings its own routine. Most of us are inevitably creatures of habit. As we can please ourselves in retirement, the routine can be far more flexible than that imposed by the discipline of work. But it is worthwhile trying to establish some kind of routine, however flexible it may be, rather than being completely haphazard in our ways.

Banish inertia

Above all, we should fight against what is aptly described as the 'scrap-heap' syndrome. The European Working Party on Retirement also commented in its Report that, 'Too often the image of the retired person in society is of one who has ceased to contribute productively to the economy, and who has earned, by his working life, a retirement period of rest and inactivity. It is not surprising then, that many retired people passively accept the role thrust upon them, and the retirement years, which should be a time of enjoyment and fulfilment, very often become an inert period.'

If you can accept, as you near retirement, that it will mean a vital adjustment in your life — a completely new and untried experience; if you can pause a while to take stock of yourself and to think about the deeper issues of life, its meaning and purpose, your place in the scheme of things and your relationships with others; if you can appreciate that your continuing development is a life-long process, and you can find a new and satisfying role in life, you are well on the way to a happy retirement.

Points to remember

1. People's attitudes to retirement and acceptance of the need

for adjustments in their way of thinking are fundamental issues.

2. Adjusting to the new pattern of living and changing in attitudes to life are difficult to achieve without conscious effort. It takes time to change the habits and attitudes of years.

3. Work not only brings income, but also purpose and objectives, status and identity, social contacts and group support, and routine and discipline in life. On retirement, people have to find other ways of satisfying these basic needs.

4. To look on retirement as providing a future of uninterrupted rest and inactivity can lead only to disappointment, boredom and ill-health. Instead, seek to find a satisfying and purposeful role in life which will make retirement a rewarding experience.

Chapter 3
Personal Relationships

Old friends, new friends

We have tried in the previous chapter to show that although
many people take their jobs for granted, work does offer
them social and psychological rewards, besides being a source
of income. Work provides a motive power which, when
abruptly switched off, can leave people suffering from
retirement shock, with no alternative driving force to sustain
them. At the very time when they need the reassurance and
counsel which friends can offer, their social circle is
contracted — they are thrust into a smaller and more
personal world. Personal relationships created for people
through their work are brought to an end by their
retirement, however much they might be determined at the
time to maintain them. Yet it is rather a futile exercise, after
retirement, to play the ghost — haunting the place where you
used to work. Of course, your old colleagues have said how
delighted they will be to see you if you can call in after you
have been retired for a while. But if you make too much of a
habit of it, you may find yourself becoming rather a nuisance.
Things will have moved on since you left and it is really far
better to live for the present and the future rather than
haunt the past. This is one aspect of retirement which cries
out for advance preparation — to seize every opportunity,
before retirement looms up too closely, to renew old
friendships, to cement existing relationships and to make
new friends outside the working environment.

However, our advice on haunting is qualified where the
employer provides special facilities for retired staff to meet
from time to time — perhaps by arranging regular social
gatherings, or the occasional coach outing or theatre visit.

This gives retired employees a chance to meet former colleagues, to discuss common problems, and to share experiences of retirement.

The family circle

A crucial element in any discussion of personal relationships and the effect of retirement upon them is the way in which they are likely to change within the immediate family circle. Achieving a satisfactory understanding plays an important part in making the vital adjustment needed if retirement is to be a rewarding experience. You have to consider not only the effect of your retirement upon yourself, but also how it will affect the lives of those closest to you. This holds good whatever your personal circumstances as a 'retired person' may be — whether married, single, divorced or widowed.

Marriage partners

Probably the majority of our readers nearing retirement are married men or women, so we ask the unmarried to forgive us if we start by offering our thoughts on the way in which a man's relationship with his wife may be affected by retirement. The points made regarding married couples may have equal relevance to, say, two sisters intending to share a retirement home together. Much of what we say can probably be applied, with adaptations, to your own particular circumstances.

In the case of some married couples, the wife may herself still be working when her husband retires. In other cases they may still have children of school age (which, incidentally, may increase the husband's State Retirement Pension). Not only do personal circumstances differ widely, but so do people's individual characters. Neither we nor our relationships fall into convenient slots.

However, in many cases the wife already spends much of her time in the home. She may have had to adjust to a retirement of her own in the past, having previously had a full-time job. Or, she may have had to face up to another, more personal, retirement — from the day-to-day work associated with motherhood. There are no longer the children to care for. Usually they will have grown up and left home by the time the husband retires.

In many ways husbands and wives lead their own separate lives before the man retires. How much time have they spent together in the past? For years the pattern for five days out of seven has probably been a hurried word or two over breakfast, and then they see nothing of each other until evening, when they join each other for dinner or supper. Perhaps they will take up the rest of the evening in watching television, or having the occasional evening out. Maybe the wife has to try not to disturb her husband while he pores over a pile of papers from the office, or he has to be content while she marks pupils' schoolwork! The weekends provide a different pattern, but here again a routine of sorts becomes established over the years.

Possibly the only occasion when the two of them spend any appreciable length of time continuously in each other's company is the annual holiday, a time they plan and prepare for carefully so that they can relax and enjoy it to the full. It is a sad reflection on our social habits that probably far more planning and preparation go into the arrangements for that summer holiday than for all the years of retirement ahead.

While the husband has been absorbed in his work, the wife has been establishing her own pattern of living. The chances are that she will have built up her own close circle of friends and will have found interests outside the home. She may, for instance, be an active member of the Women's Institute or Townswomen's Guild, may enjoy bridge with three other ladies, and put in a day's voluntary work for the Red Cross, as well as coping with shopping.

In fact, the man's retirement can have as great an effect on his wife as it does on himself. It is a time for special tolerance, patience and understanding. Above all, it calls for early discussion and general agreement on what is to be the new pattern of life for both. They must be strong enough to sustain a shared relationship which will be closer than any they have previously experienced in their marriage. A husband usually has more to learn. Perhaps he has previously spent his energies in being the main breadwinner of the family, and has tended to take the wife's caring role for granted. Now he has to give support and understanding so that their relationship grows closer through the newly shared experience.

One lesson he must learn is that he should not expect his wife to give up her own friends and outside interests just because he has retired. As individuals we should all be free to pursue our own special interests and we all need our solitude from time to time.

It may be that occasionally you will come across a retired couple who wish for nothing more than to spend every moment of their time happily together and who share all interests in common. Such devotion is rare, and the tragedy of it is that barring accident or other disaster, they are unlikely to die at the same time; one will be left to struggle on. If they had each built up their own circles of friends and had encouraged each other to have separate interests outside the home, the bereaved one might find solace more easily.

Men sometimes need reminding that while their word might have been law at work, home has for long been the wife's territory. There, she has been the boss. The man who, having nothing better to do with his time, decides to exercise all his proven organising ability in the kitchen, will probably achieve one of two things. He will either provoke a short sharp retaliation and hastily give up the idea, or he may in time unwittingly so destroy his wife's self-confidence that she finally takes to her bed suffering from various symptoms which may be attributed to the chronic disease of 'displaced housewife'. If that happens, he will certainly need all his organising ability. A crash course in cookery might also be helpful! On the other hand, our warnings to the organisation-and-methods man should not be quoted as a justification for leaving all the housework to his wife, nor should she take our words as a warning that it is wise to make him keep out of her way when she is working about the home. No. This is a sphere in which there is scope for mutual tolerance and understanding. Being in each other's company for longer each day should not mean being in each other's way.

Of course, if he doesn't know what to do with himself all day, he is likely to become a nuisance, disrupting his wife's routine of housework with his idle chatter. He may become over-anxious to help and only succeed in getting in the way. Then, if she finds him jobs to keep him occupied he may feel perversely that he is nothing more than an unpaid home-help!

For the wife whose children have grown up and no longer

live at home, the old routine of housework may have become a chore which she no longer enjoys. On the other hand, for some wives, cleanliness and orderliness in the home become almost an obsession. In either event, she is unlikely to welcome her newly retired husband trudging in from the garden with muddy boots, or scattering his belongings about the house as, grasshopper-like, he hops from one vague interest to another!

Much of what we have said depends upon the individual personalities of the persons involved. Sharp differences in temperament, which attracted couples to each other in their youth, sometimes become intensified as the years go by, and no longer appear so endearing. Tolerance and understanding must once again be the main ingredients in achieving a satisfactory relationship in the new situation. Failure to adjust successfully to the new situation has in some cases resulted in retired persons seeking a divorce. In those instances marriages survived while the husband was at work, but without give and take the partners could not successfully share the increased hours together brought about by retirement.

Perhaps the ideal balance is reached when each can be busily engaged about his or her own activities and interests during the day, yet having time also to come together to enjoy each other's companionship; each ready to show interest in what the other has been doing, and each ready to help the other if needs be.

Single people

We hope that we have offered some food for thought to married couples concerned with the prospects of retirement. We believe that much of what we have said can also be applied to single people, whether they are bachelors, spinsters, divorcees, widows or widowers. The same tolerance and understanding is needed in adjusting their relationships with others who will be close to them in their daily lives when retirement arrives, whether they be relatives or friends who will be sharing the retirement years. Whatever the circumstances, acceptance of the special need for understanding, discussion and mutual adjustments is self-evident.

There are an estimated 300,000 single women in this

country caring for elderly relatives, and there is no doubt
that many single women have the double task of trying to
cope with a job during the day and also caring for an elderly
relative. Perhaps their first reaction is that the load will
lighten when retirement comes. Retirement normally presents
a person with another 2,000 hours a year of leisure time.
Of course, a single woman in these circumstances will want to
spend more time in caring for the elderly relative. But we do
stress that she should also try to preserve friendships and
outside interests and if possible develop them further, so far
as circumstances permit. An organisation directly concerned
with such problems is The National Council for the Single
Woman and her Dependants.

Living alone

So far, we have not spoken of the very many people who are
living alone when they reach retirement age, although we have
pointed out the dangers of becoming a 'four-walled' person.
A conscious effort (and it *is* an effort) has to be made to seek
new interests and friendships outside the home, fostering
existing friendships and renewing old ones. If, then, you have
no home to share with friend or family when you retire, but
will be living alone, you have to make up your mind whether
you will be content with your own company, especially at a
time when you have lost the companionship you enjoyed at
work and the sense of purpose and security which your job
provided. We hope that you will have prepared in good time
beforehand for your retirement and so will have at your
disposal a range of leisure activities and many friends outside
the home. If this is the case, as well as enjoying a greater sense
of freedom and the change in pace, you will adapt quickly
and smoothly to the new way of life alone. You may value the
chance to be on your own — there can certainly be a
difference between just being alone and feeling lonely. If on
the other hand, you fear loneliness, *now* is the time to
consider whether there is any way in which you can find
companionship in your retirement. Perhaps you could come
to a sharing arrangement with a relative or a good friend —
maybe a temporary arrangement at first to see how it will
work out. Other possibilities regarding living arrangements
are dealt with in chapter 8. More and more voluntary bodies

are providing housing schemes intended to meet the needs of single people. Some of the arrangements are specially geared for retired people.

Be a good neighbour

This chapter has been primarily concerned with close personal and family relationships, but in our daily lives we come into contact with many other people. Our chapter on part-time work (Chapter 7) deals with voluntary service, which is one of the ways in which people coming to retirement can discover new interests and at the same time satisfy a need to feel that they are still useful and participating members of the community. Of course, not everyone wants to join a voluntary organisation. But you don't have to *join* anything to be a good neighbour. In 1977, David Ennals, Secretary of State for Social Services, launched the 'Good Neighbour' campaign. As he said:

' "We all want to be good neighbours. We want to help when we see an elderly woman struggling with heavy shopping, a disabled man making his way painfully through the snow, a bereaved and lonely wife or husband. There are so many things that we could do to help. But sometimes we hold back for what seems to us the best of reasons. We're afraid of invading other people's privacy, worried that proud and independent old people may snub us, too shy to make the first move." He asked people to act on that impulse to help, as "however good we try to make our social services, they cannot do everything that is needed." There are many ways in which we can be a good neighbour to the sick, the elderly, the handicapped, the housebound and others in trouble or difficulty.

A leaflet issued by the Department of Health and Social Security suggests we should help people to help themselves. Many people want to remain independent and to stay in their own homes as long as they possibly can. But because of age or sickness, their ability to look after themselves may diminish. If a husband is sick a wife may become ill too from the strain of looking after him. One or both may become housebound.

What can you do to help? You can visit and talk to them. The family may be scattered — sons and daughters may live hundreds of miles away and be able to visit only infrequently. Be a good listener and you will win their respect and confidence.

You can help with shopping. Many people — particularly those who live some distance from the shops — find it painful to walk there and confusing to shop in bustling supermarkets and self-service stores. Others are confined to their homes.

You can cook a meal for them. Some people may be too frail to cook for themselves regularly.

You can see that they are warm in winter. People are more prone to illness, especially respiratory infections, in winter — and old and sick people suffer the effects of cold more than most.

You can care for the disabled. Many disabled and handicapped people overcome their difficulties with great courage. They do not waste time in regrets, but are determined to live as normal a life as possible. Yet their disadvantages are great.

You can help in other ways. If you are a car owner, can you give them a lift to the shops, the station, the hospital? For the housebound, a trip to the countryside or to the sea? Can you give other practical help — change a fuse, fix a plug? Move some furniture? Help with decorating or in the garden, clean the windows, clear the path of snow in winter? Help to fill in forms?

You can look out for distress signals. You can help by being on the alert for emergencies. Don't be afraid to find out if anything is wrong.

Finally, remember it is not all one-sided. In helping your neighbour you could yourself find much satisfaction and perhaps receive help yourself.'   (Quoted from *Choice* magazine.)

A new role

In *As You Like It* William Shakespeare wrote that, 'All the World's a stage, And all the men and women merely players'.

You may have noticed how easily children slip into a world of fantasy — the little girl as she plays nurse to her dolls or the boy dreaming that he is the sheriff, brandishing his six-gun and hot on the trail of the outlaw band. In the adult world, too, people tend to adopt roles which they feel to be appropriate to their way of life. A person will try to fulfil a particular role in order to meet *other people's expectations*, and this will also affect their personal relationships. For instance, there is the salesman who must be the life and soul of the party, ever ready with the merry quip; the ex-army man who preserves his military bearing, complete with clipped moustache and cavalry twill trousers; the undergraduate with the patched jeans, long hair and trailing college scarf; or the lady executive, impeccably dressed and groomed — the epitome of cool efficiency. In truth our impressions of these characters, and of people in many other walks of life are largely created for us by actors and comedians who play those larger-than-life characters of radio, TV screen and theatre. In the same way, the media have created the popular impression of the retired person. How are retired people portrayed in this world of make-believe? Let's see — there

are the Darby and Joans, enjoying a good old sing-song at
the OAP club (the piano is never in tune); there is the old
chap living with his son and daughter-in-law — making a
nuisance of himself at times but very fond of the
grandchildren; there is the elderly spinster who cannot bear
to have anything out of place in her little flat and is always
making a fuss of her cats or the budgie.

The scriptwriters and actors make these characters figures
of fun, joy, or sadness, as they please. But remember, when
you retire you do not have to fall into one of these
recognised roles. Beware the stereotype of the poor old
pensioner with nothing much to do and too much time to
do it in! It is not really a requirement of society that you
should while away your time sitting on a park bench or in the
shelter on the promenade.

There is another distinction to be made. This is in the
roles people play during their working lives. Whether we think
of them under the label of solicitor, accountant, secretary,
housewife or mother, we are seeing them in clearly defined
roles which have a specific meaning and purpose in society.
A retired person, however, has no defined role. The title
bestows no new set of standards or pattern of behaviour.
No rules are laid down, or objectives set out. It is a label
that covers the whole spectrum of society and provides only
one link — the accident of age.

Make your status as a retired person merely an incidental
adjunct to some other, more active, role of your own
choosing: a role which will restore the sense of purpose
which you lost on retirement.

Perhaps one day some genius will invent a new word for
retirement which will liberate its image from the inherited
views which still persist in people's minds. In grandfather's
day 'retirement' was for the old and decrepit; the people
who were on the scrap-heap and no longer fit for work.
Nowadays most people retiring are still vigorous and healthy,
with many years of active life ahead, but the old image is
slow to change. A glance at those 'best wishes in your
retirement' cards on the shelves of the gift card shops will
show that most of them perpetuate the view that the recipient
will have 'earned a good rest', or can 'put his feet up at last'.
Why can't they create a more positive image, more closely
modelled on the Spanish term for retirement, which speaks

for itself: *Preparación a la Jubilación* — preparation for the jubilation!

In your working life you have played a role in which much of the script has been written by others. In retirement you have to write your own script and to act out your part. If, with Shakespeare, you can think of life as a stage and yourself as a player, then your retirement means you are at the beginning of Act Three. Give a good performance!

Seeking advice

We cannot over-emphasise the importance of trying to construct a sound base for future personal relationships in preparing for the new phase in life. This is perhaps the most vital adjustment, requiring all your care and understanding if you are to make a success of the future. It is worthwhile remembering too, that whatever the problem, whether it is concerned with personal relationships or with other aspects of retirement, there is always somewhere you can go for advice. Seek it out — get expert help, rather than let your worries grow too great. If you don't know where to go for the advice you need, a good starting point is always the local Citizens' Advice Bureau, where trained helpers are available to set you on the right road. If you need specialist guidance, the CAB office will not only know the nearest office of the required organisation but in many cases can even tell you the name of the actual person to contact there.

Points to remember

1. As retirement approaches it is wise to build up friendships away from the working environment.
2. Retirement affects not only you, but the lives of all those in the immediate family circle. It calls for special tolerance, patience and understanding between marriage partners. The same applies to single people and their relationships with others close to them.
3. Living alone may not mean loneliness, but this could come unless a conscious effort is made to seek new interests and to establish friendships outside the home.
4. There is danger in meekly accepting the stereotyped role of the pensioner. Those who retire successfully create new, purposeful roles for themselves which are not dependent upon their retired status.

Chapter 4
Money Matters

Introduction

The Western world is a finance-oriented society, and in that context retirement brings us to one of the most important watersheds in our lives. When we arrive at this age most of us suffer a fall in income, but too many people worry and brood over the problem before retirement, without attempting to analyse each specific point which bothers them. If you are in that situation you are expecting a reduction in your post-retirement income, but have you worked out what will be the difference between your gross income — pre-retirement and post-retirement? More important, what will be the difference in *net* income? Here, surely, is the key. You will not enjoy such a large gross income in retirement but you will pay less tax, no National Insurance contributions, less travelling costs, and at 60 or 65, as appropriate, you will collect the State Retirement Pension plus, possibly, an occupational pension of some sort from your employer. Worrying in a general way about finance cannot help you. A little later we are going to give an example of one way in which you can take an analytical approach. If the situation is truly depressing, then you can consider what remedial action is necessary. The earlier you tackle the problem before retirement, the better.

In assessing a person's liability for income tax, the Inspector automatically sets off the appropriate personal allowance against total income. When the person reaches 65 years of age, the higher age allowance takes the place of the personal allowance. People with little income other than the State Retirement Pension benefit considerably. If total income is above the amount currently determined by government, the age allowance is reduced by £2 for every £3 of income above the limit, until it is reduced to the normal personal allowance. In general terms, for a married couple the income tax age allowance keeps pace with the State Retirement Pension. But remember, the State Retirement Pension is *not* tax free, and even if you have no other income you may still have to complete an income tax return.

Income

Let us look at the figures of a fictitious Mr Smith shortly to to retire, and build up a picture of his pre-retirement and post-retirement situation. We print a budget on page 48 (Schedule A). The first and obvious piece of information for the picture is Mr Smith's present salary — say £6,000, which he would insert in Column A. During a career of 40 years he spent the last 30 years in an organisation which has a pension scheme that provides a pension based on 1/60th of present salary for each year of service. This will produce a pension of 30/60ths or one half of £6,000 = £3,000. In this example, Mr Smith would insert for Item 2 (Column B) post-retirement occupational pension = £3,000.

It is essential that you understand exactly how you will benefit from the occupational pension scheme. We suggest that you read your pension fund handbook or guide. Most employers now produce one for pension fund members. Some of these books are full of jargon; a few are intelligible. But nearly all pension managers are sympathetic and readily approachable. (If they were not, it is unlikely that they would have reached their present position.) In the past, trade unions have been accused of devoting too much time to the weekly pay packet, but of late there has been increasing recognition of the fact that an occupational pension is part of the remuneration package and in reality constitutes deferred pay. Fortunately, an increasing number of employers will give their employees an annual estimate of their pension entitlement.

If you are a married man, establish what happens to the pension if you die before your wife. Please be practical and let her know what provision is made under the scheme for a surviving wife and/or dependants.

Before retirement age is reached, you may have the

opportunity to forego a proportion of your annual occupational pension and take a lump sum instead. You may well wish to take the opportunity to commute part of your pension in this way so as to have a capital sum in order to carry out repairs or improvements to your home, to visit friends or relations overseas, to help your children, or for any combination of objectives. Your state of health is a prime factor in making the decision. You may prefer to have a useful capital sum at your disposal now, rather than the prospect of a full pension for the rest of your life. You may prefer to take the lump sum (usually limited to a maximum, equivalent to 18 months of your final salary), to indulge yourself to a certain extent and use the balance to buy an annuity. By taking a lump sum, the pension is decreased and any future increase in the pension to allow for inflation will also be lost on the proportion of pension commuted. Take professional advice regarding the investment of the lump sum in, say, an annuity. Generally speaking, a purchased life annuity will produce a substantially higher net income than net pension given up for cash.

If you send a stamped addressed envelope to the Pre-Retirement Association, they will send you a list of investment advisers and life assurance brokers who are members of the Association and who can give advice on planning your financial affairs in retirement.

The next item on our list is any other earned income, such as fees for part-time work. Imagine that our potential pensioner, Mr Smith, has been in touch with the local education authority which was advertising for lecturers. He has a guarantee of teaching his particular subject at the adult education centre and may expect this to produce an annual income of £300 per annum, as well as providing an outside interest in retirement. (We develop other ideas for part-time work in Chapter 7.) He will therefore insert £300 in Column B, Item No 3.

Many people still refer to the State Retirement Pension as the Old Age Pension. This term should always be firmly resisted. 'Old age' is an offensive term, and you must not be labelled 'old' because of government terminology. The correct title is the State Retirement Pension and this has been so for the last 30 years. (It is, by the way, equally incorrect to refer to Employment Offices or Jobcentres as Labour Exchanges.)

The basic pension is only payable in full if you have a good contributions record. If, for example, you have worked overseas for a number of years without exercising your option to pay for your stamps, then your pension will be reduced. You can write to the Ministry of Pensions and National Insurance in Newcastle to ascertain your contribution record. In that case always quote your National Insurance number.

If you have ever dashed into a post office to buy a few stamps, only to be confronted by a long queue of pensioners, it may be of interest to know that you can exercise the option to receive a cheque at home instead, every fourth or 13th week, in arrears. The DHSS will not make a direct payment to your bank account.

If you can choose your last day at work, make it a Wednesday. You will be eligible to receive the State Retirement Pension from Thursday which will be your new 'pay day'.

The basic state pension may be increased by one or two supplements. If you have worked beyond 60 (women) or 65 (men), a small amount will be added to the basic amount. Another small increment will be due in respect of Graduated Pension contributions. Let us assume that Mr Smith is married, and speaking in annual terms, his state pension is worth £1,600 per annum. He will write this in Column B of the budget, Item No 4.

After years of procrastination by the state, the new state pension scheme came into existence in April 1978, and the first benefits will be payable from April 1979. It will, regrettably, be some years before the earnings-related pension makes any tangible addition to the present basic state scheme.

The new state scheme has two tiers. For weekly earnings up to £15 the scheme provides a 100 per cent pension. For earnings between £15 and £105 a week, the scheme will provide a pension of 25 per cent. Earnings over and above the £105 limit will not attract an additional pension. Those who retire within the next 20 years will receive only a proportionate pension. The basic pension is revalued annually.

Fortunately, one of the effects of the new state pension scheme has been to force employers to take a good look at their existing pension schemes. If they decided to opt out of the new pension scheme, then their schemes had to offer equivalent or superior benefits.

Investments and rents

Later on in this chapter we go into the various types of investment in some detail. A regular re-appraisal of the opportunities open to investors is recommended, and a good clear examination is essential at the date of retirement, when so many other changes take place.

For the current exercise, we shall assume that Mr Smith's investment is held in a building society share account jointly with his wife. This produces £500 per annum after deduction of tax at the basic rate of 33 per cent. He will write in £500 for Item No 5 in both Columns A and B. (The joint account allows both partners to draw from the building society; this is useful in times of emergency.)

There is no other income in respect of rents received and so Mr Smith tots up Columns A and B. He finds his gross income will decrease by £1,100 from £6,500 to £5,400.

The real pay-off comes when he examines the deductions to be made from his income. He will cease to pay National Insurance contributions (£210 pa), and employees' superannuation contributions (£300 pa). His tax bill will drop by approximately £550 pa, ie from £1,413 to £865. Had he not enjoyed such a good pension, on reaching his 65th birthday he would have become eligible for age allowance for the whole of the tax year. (We have tried to keep specific references to actual figures for tax rates and allowances to a minimum because of the propensity of Chancellors to revise these more often than a general book on retirement can deal with.) For current information, inexpensive paperbacks to be recommended are *Money and Your Retirement* (published by the Pre-Retirement Association and *Choice* magazine) and *The Daily Mail Income Tax Guide.* For general rules, you can obtain free of charge from your local income tax office the booklet *Income Tax and the Elderly* (leaflet IR4).

Our pensioner finds that his net annual income has only decreased by about £40. Because he no longer has to travel to work and keep up appearances to the same extent, his real income represented by pounds in the pocket means an improvement in his circumstances. Unfortunately, many other pensioners benefited too late in life from occupational pension schemes, or retired before their introduction. This applies particularly to manual workers. For this reason we talk later about supplementary benefits. You may also be able to assist older persons who, through misplaced pride or failure to understand benefits available, do not claim their rights from the state. (According to a 1978 study conducted by the Supplementary Benefits Commission, nearly £300 million is not being claimed by those entitled to financial assistance.)

We have now sketched on a broad canvas a method of judging how one's income will compare during the run-up to retirement and in retirement.

Expenditure

We next ask you to take a look at your expenditure, and again measure pre-retirement and post-retirement differences. Some items will remain unchanged but try to picture your new life-style: no travelling to work, more leisure, more time to spend with your family in the home and greater freedom in the choice of holidays. This new life pattern will result in higher costs due to increased lighting, heating and food in the home, offset by reduced travelling expenses and travel concessions.

If you can produce some home grown vegetables in retirement from your greenhouse, garden or allotment, this will be another saving. If you hire a colour TV set, enquire if the local companies offer special terms to pensioners. Other points we would like to make are:

TRAVEL
If both partners in a marriage travel to work then obviously savings will be made. If you have enjoyed the use of a company car, then your expenditure will go up, although income tax on the use of the car will cease. Depending on where you live you may be entitled to concession travel on local transport. Presumably you have put aside savings for a replacement vehicle if you have decided you will continue in retirement to run a car. If you are some way off retirement, explore the possibilities of your employer selling you the car

you have been using, if it is not too large a vehicle to run economically. Companies are always changing the vehicles in their fleet. (A word to the transport manager in good time before your retirement may result in an opportunity to buy the car you are currently using or another company car at a discounted price.)

You can buy a British Rail Senior Citizens' Rail Card which offers half-price travel for longer journeys. (Cost £7.00 at 1978 prices or £3.50 for away day journeys only.)

FOOD AND HEATING

You must allow more for food and heating, because you will be spending more time in the home. If you have been receiving luncheon vouchers or eating a mid-day meal in a subsidised staff restaurant/dining room, then your own expenditure must go up as you lose these facilities. (You may find, after retirement, that a senior citizens' club locally can offer you a cooked lunch at a nominal figure.) Experience shows, however, that where both partners have been going out to work, there is a greater temptation to buy expensive convenience or frozen foods. The average housewife will welcome the opportunity to return to less expensive and more conventional forms of cooking. Lighting and heating bills at home will increase also, with your increased domestic presence.

RATE REBATES ETC

We have written about rate rebates, rent rebates and rent allowances in chapter 8.

We have produced two schedules: Schedule A shows the gross annual income less the compulsory deductions for income tax, National Insurance and superannuation. Schedule B shows the main items of expenditure which comprise the costs to be met in a domestic budget. Schedule B is for the items under your personal control. It is always a salutary exercise to examine in detail where money is being spent, in case opportunities for economies exist. (To be truly effective, the budget must be compiled honestly and meticulously!)

When you have completed this exercise, you can make a comparison between your estimated expenditure and your estimated net annual income.

Schedule A

Gross annual income	A Before retirement (£ pa)	B After retirement (£ pa)
1. Salary		
2. Occupational pension		
3. Fees		
4. State Retirement and Graduated Pension		
5. Investment income		
6. Other (eg rents)		
TOTAL		
Deduct:		
7. Income tax		
8. National Insurance contributions		
9. Employee's superannuation contributions		
Total net annual income	£	£
Less: Net expenditure brought forward from detailed schedule. (See Schedule B)		
TOTAL	£	£

Schedule B

The main items of the domestic budget should include:

Expenditure	Before retirement (£ pa)	After retirement (£ pa)
Food Home consumption, including entertainment Lunches/dinners away from home Staff restaurant lunches/senior citizens' clubs		
Transport Car running costs, ie petrol/oil/repairs/tax Public transport/British Rail Card		
Entertainment TV hire purchase or hire/licence Theatre/cinema/concerts Sports/hobbies/competitions		
Leisure Magazines/newspapers/book clubs Adult education classes Holidays Garden (tools/seeds/greenhouse/mower) Townswomen's Guilds/Women's Institutes		
Personal Clothes Chemist/prescriptions/dentist Subscriptions, clubs/associations Hairdresser Drinks/tobacco Football pools/lotteries/raffles Dry cleaning, shoe repairs Postage/stationery		
Gifts Children/grandchildren Birthdays and Christmas Weddings		
Donations Charities/Church		

House
Rates — general
     — water
Mortgage/rent
Insurance — house and contents/personal
    effects and all risks
Repairs/maintenance/DIY
Gas
Electricity
Telephone
Fuel
Oil
Detergents/soap/cleaning materials		

Savings/Insurance Endowment policies		
Pets Food, veterinary fees, dog licence		
TOTAL	£	£

You now have a guide to your post-retirement budget. We hope that the exercise has had two effects: firstly, to assist you to clear your own mind and, secondly, to give you a more factual appreciation of what your financial position is likely to be in retirement. Also it will identify your tax rate, which is essential in making investment decisions.

If there is a gap, then you can consider ways and means to bridge it. Various alternatives exist:

1. *To increase income:*
   (a) You can consider finding another job (part-time or full-time) after retirement. (See chapter 7, in which we also discuss the earnings rule.)
   (b) Your investments might be re-deployed to produce a greater net yield (eg if you do not pay income tax then do not keep any money in a building society).
   (c) You may be able to raise, at a later date, an additional income by means of a mortgage annuity on your home. (See chapter 8.)

2. *To decrease expenditure:*
   (a) Is a car an essential or is it now a luxury? Would it be cheaper just to hire a self-drive car for holidays and special events? A small new car will tie up at least £2,800 of precious capital (which could be invested) plus £120 per annum for tax and insurance before you have put the first gallon of petrol in the tank.
   (b) Avoid taking your holiday at the height of the season, and take off-peak holidays to enjoy the very economical long-term winter breaks which are arranged by specialists in travel for pensioners — for example, Saga Holidays.
   (c) Take advantage of all concessions open to pensioners. These will include:
      (i) Reduced or free bus travel in some areas. Cheap fares on London's underground.
      (ii) Free NHS prescriptions. (Simply sign the back of the prescription form when you take it to the chemist.) Elastic hosiery and drugs supplied by the outpatients department of hospitals are also free to pensioners.
      (iii) Reduced rates for classes at adult education centres. For example many colleges charge retirement

pensioners half the normal course fee, and may remit the fee entirely for those receiving supplementary benefit.

(iv) The local Citizens' Advice Bureau and the Social Services departments can advise on local Meals on Wheels and Home Help services. You may not need these regularly but they can be invaluable in times of illness.

(v) You will probably be entitled to the use of local authority swimming baths at reduced rates or even free. Swimming is an excellent exercise, particularly for back pain sufferers.

(vi) You can visit over 700 ancient monuments under the control of the Department of Environment at reduced prices. Similar privileges are offered by the National Trust.

(vii) Your local cinema will give details of reduced rates for pensioners.

(viii) Your public library may excuse you from fines imposed on overdue books. If you are ill or handicapped, ring your local library as some authorities operate mobile libraries or can arrange for books to be delivered to those confined to their beds.

(ix) Dry cleaning and hairdressing establishments often offer discounts to pensioners.

Bank accounts

(a) CLEARING BANKS

Do not let your cash accumulate in an ordinary account beyond the level necessary to avoid bank charges. If, like most of us, you are lazy you can, on your next visit to the bank, switch the surplus to a deposit account. If you have an unexpected emergency you are only required to give seven days' notice to transfer money back to your current account. In the meantime, the money in your deposit account will be earning interest. Tax on the interest is not deducted at source.

(b) NATIONAL SAVINGS BANK

If you have retired to a village, then the local post office may be more convenient for some transactions than your ordinary bank account. Interest on an ordinary savings account is tax-free for the first £70. The interest rate payable is normally unattractive for anything larger than a small emergency reserve.

An NSB deposit account pays a higher rate of interest, without any tax-free interest. One month's notice is required for withdrawals.

(c) TRUSTEE SAVINGS BANK

At present, TSB savings accounts pay the first £70 of interest free of tax. Interest on all National Savings Bank and TSB accounts is aggregated for individuals up to the maximum of £70. Currently the TSB interest rate is lower than that paid by the National Savings Bank ordinary account. Note, however, that it is anticipated that the tax concession enjoyed by the TSBs will cease on 1st November 1979.

(d) LOCAL AUTHORITY BONDS

If you have funds to invest for a minimum of one year upwards, a secure home for them can be found with local authorities. The Saturday *Daily Telegraph* quotes current offers. Remember it is not normally possible to withdraw funds before the end of the contracted period. Tax at the basic rate is deducted at source.

Professional advice

The earlier you carry out the budget operation we have suggested the more time you will have before retirement to juggle your assets and to distribute, if need be, your financial eggs between different baskets. It is also probable that while you are employed, it may be easier for you to seek the advice of professional experts. If, over the years, you have, in your business or professional capacity, dealt with a member of the accountancy, banking, insurance, building society or legal professions, then you may have ready access to the ear of a financial expert whose judgement you can trust. Now that you have some idea of your assets and your financial situation, let us broadly outline the various choices open to you, so that if necessary you may approach an expert in the particular field that interests you. There are very few specialist firms of personal financial planners, so if you are in doubt write to the PRA, as we suggested earlier in this chapter. Usually, insurance brokers do not charge fees because they collect their commission from the company whose policy or annuity you decide to purchase. Your local bank manager may not have at his fingertips all the information needed to give your financial position a complete overhaul. To meet the need, Barclays bank has set up a Money Doctor service and Midland bank a Personal Financial Counselling service. A fee is charged for both services.

Some stockbrokers will not be very interested unless you have many thousands of pounds to play with on the Stock Exchange. Small investors bring them little profit in the way of commission. However, the Stock Exchange is anxious to attract the small investor and will send a list of brokers willing to act for you. But small share holdings are much more of a gamble because the risk is not spread wide enough. Unit trusts are the answer for the man or woman of average means. They spread the investment over a wide and safe field. The unit trust management companies will quote one price in selling you units and another, lower, price in buying them back, and there are tax advantages.

Today, it may be taken that £25,000 is the minimum sum needed to attract the attention of firms offering a specialist share management service to individuals. Ours is a self-service age, and so the greater interest you take in the financial world, the better equipped you will be to put questions to the adviser you have selected. In the past, governments presented their Budgets once a year, but now we suffer from extra emergency Budgets, and problems are complicated by the resulting changes in VAT and income tax legislation. Inflation, the greatest worry for pensioners, is here to stay. For those who wish to keep abreast of developments, there is the monthly magazine *Pre-Retirement Choice* which is the only magazine for retirement planning. Its pages contain regular articles aimed at readers approaching retirement, and it offers a highly professional reader service. As a guide to the ever-changing financial opportunities open to savers, current returns on investments are tabulated in the *Daily Telegraph* on Saturdays ('Savers Choice'), in the *Sunday Times* ('Savings Counter') and the *Observer*. Examples given include National Savings, building societies, banks (clearing houses, Giro, Trustee and National Savings) and the finance houses.

'Money Mail' is good reading in the Wednesday issue of the *Daily Mail.* We do not suggest that you should take all these newspapers, but the dailies are available in the reading room of your local library.

Save as you earn (SAYE)

If you have five or more years to go before retirement, take a look at the two SAYE schemes currently open to investors. The National Savings Department offers a plan by which the saver undertakes to make a monthly investment of a minimum of £4 (Third Index Related Issue) for five years. The maximum investment under this scheme is £20 per month. The yield is linked to the Retail Prices Index, and if you do not draw it out for two additional years after the five years to which you are committed, a bonus equivalent to two months' contribution is added to the yield. You can withdraw from the contract before the five years is up but if you do so after the first year you will obtain 6 per cent interest. A SAYE scheme (not index related) is operated by the building societies. The current return on the building societies' scheme is 8.3 per cent (five years) or 8.6 per cent (seven years). Check with the local office of your building society.

These SAYE schemes represent a form of saving which is free from all income and capital gains tax. Provided you can commit yourself for five or seven years to a regular saving pattern, you do not technically have to be earning over any part of the period.

National Savings Certificates

These certificates are of particular interest to higher rate tax payers who should take up their full entitlement. The current issue (14th) gives a tax free yield ranging from 6 per cent (one year) to 9.39 per cent in year four. This averages over the four year span to 7.59 per cent. You can invest up to £3,000 in this issue.

Many people are sitting on certificates issued years ago. We do urge you to see what you have, and compare earlier yields with those now obtainable. You can get the leaflet P156W from the post office which gives details of interest payable on earlier issues. You may even find that you are still holding

Issue number 1 which returns an historic rate of interest at the princely figure of less than one-and-a-half per cent! This is legal daylight robbery and as you approach retirement you cannot afford to subsidise the government so lavishly!

Building societies

A person whose income is so low that he or she does not pay income tax in retirement should not keep any money in a building society. Tax is taken before you get the interest, and it cannot be reclaimed. If you wish to invest in a building society, choose one of the larger well known societies which is a member of the Building Societies Association, and enjoying trustee security status. A building society is an ideal place for that emergency reserve which we all need as our umbrella for the proverbial rainy day, while still giving a reasonable return in interest. If one Saturday morning, when you are short of cash, you find that your children and grandchildren are about to descend on you for the weekend, then (unlike the clearing banks) you will be able to collect cash across the counter.

Make sure that the emergency reserve in your ordinary building society account is not too large. It is easy to switch the excess into a longer-term investment which is currently producing 0.5 per cent more than the ordinary share account.

Retirement Issue: National Savings Certificates

These certificates are such good value that the government allows purchasers to hold only £700 each. They can be bought in units of £10. Notwithstanding their title they can be bought by men aged 65 plus and women of 60 plus whether they have retired or not. These certificates are index-linked so that as the General Index of Retail Prices goes up, so does the value of your investment. In addition, if you hold them for five years you receive 4 per cent interest. The increased value and the interest are both free of income tax and Capital Gains tax. If you have to encash the certificates after one year you receive the benefit of index linking, but not of the 4 per cent bonus. £500 invested in the certificates in June 1975 and sold in September 1978 produced over £767, ie before the bonus payable after five years. We hope the level of inflation suffered in recent years will not return, but until inflation is permanently reduced to well below its current level we think these certificates are not to be missed.

The financial pages of some Sunday newspapers often contain a chart of current values, and are well worth a few minutes of study. As well as this, the main post offices display the monthly Retail Prices Index. If you think you might at some time be eligible for a rent or rates rebate, it is useful to know that these certificates are ignored for purposes of calculating income.

Stock up before retirement

Mrs Margaret Thatcher attracted considerable attention some years ago when an article in *Choice* magazine reported her advice to people approaching retirement that they should build up a store cupboard of non-perishable foods. As a grocer's daughter, her advice, in a period of continuing inflation, remains sound, although we are not advocating the stockpiling of goods in short supply which only inflates the price.

Apart from food, we suggest you take a look around the house before retirement and replace all the expensive household items of equipment which are nearing the end of their economic lives. Refrigerators, washing machines, tumble dryers and vacuum cleaners are obvious examples. A portable TV for the bedroom or kitchen is a luxury to treat yourself to while you are still enjoying a full income. Unless you have access to ample free or cheap supplies of fruit and vegetables, the economics of a large freezer for a retired couple are dubious. Power cuts and the need to insure the freezer's contents are an unnecessary burden unless you really have bought your retirement cottage in a remote area.

Supplementary pension

Approximately one person in four who draws the state Retirement Pension also claims supplementary benefit. It is estimated that, in addition, one person in eight is entitled to claim but fails to do so. Many older pensioners seem to feel that acceptance of supplementary benefits has a stigma attached to it. This attitude should be firmly resisted. We all make our contributions to the state's coffers during our working life. Although these benefits do not go into a separate fund the benefits should be claimed by those in need. Savings up to £1,250 are ignored, and the whole procedure is completely confidential. Arrangements can be made, where necessary, for the Department of Health and Social Security representative to visit the pensioner at home. Forms can be collected at the local DHSS office or the post office, and the Citizens' Advice Bureau will willingly assist in their completion if necessary. Readers who know of old relatives and friends living in straitened circumstances should encourage those living below the poverty line to claim their entitlement.

OVER-80s

At the age of 80 your basic State Retirement Pension is 'topped up'.

For those few people who have no right to the State Retirement Pension because they lack a contribution record, then an 'over-80s' pension, at a lower rate than the basic State Retirement Pension, becomes payable.

Shares with perks

Many retired people take a great deal of interest in the stock market. They now have the time to study comparative yields and may well have bought shares during their working lives. For those who enjoy watching the vicissitudes of the stock market, the stockbrokers Seymour Pierce & Co have published a list of concessionary discounts available to shareholders in UK companies. In retirement, if you intend to take your car across the Channel regularly, it may pay you to take a look at the shares of European Ferries. Buying 300 ordinary shares will enable you to receive up to 50 per cent discount on some of their cross-channel ferries. Discounts on men's clothing are offered to shareholders in Moss Brothers, J Hepworth and the Gieves Group. You might even be eligible for two tickets for the price of one to cross the Atlantic on the Queen Elizabeth by buying shares in Trafalgar House. These discounts are good for the companies, since it is in their own interests to make their products and services better known.

Seymour Pierce & Co are to be congratulated on their enterprise. They very properly warn punters that share price fluctuations *can* outweigh the benefits of a discount, so do not ignore these facts of life if you are tempted by the prospect of discounts on services ranging from holiday hotels to dry cleaning.

Send 20p postal order or cheque to Seymour Pierce & Co for their leaflet.

Individual pension arrangements

We have written mainly so far for the benefit of those employed in fairly large organisations. We should like now to turn to those who may be directors and/or employed by small firms. Life assurance companies operate pension schemes aimed at supplementing the benefits payable under the new state pension scheme. Provided entry to the occupational schemes is started at least 10 years before the date of retirement a pension can be provided equal to two thirds of final remuneration. A tax-free lump sum may be taken in lieu of part of the pension. The maximum lump sum payable is usually equivalent to one-and-a-half times the final annual salary. The employer must contribute to the scheme. Cover can also be provided for death in service and for a widow. The pension consultants referred to page 43 can be relied upon to give good professional service.

The self-employed

The government has allowed valuable tax concessions to be offered to those people who do not fall within the scope of a company pension scheme. Within certain limits, each pension contribution is eligible for tax relief at the highest rate of tax paid on earned income. The pension received is taxed as earned income, and thus escapes the investment income surcharge. A proportion of the retirement fund built up may be paid as a tax-free lump sum. You can choose your own date of retirement at any age between 60 and 75. The investment of the contributions is totally exempt from tax.

Some schemes allow considerable flexibility, including provision to cease contributions for any one year, which is a useful escape hatch for the self-employed man who may suffer a poor year's trading. No business man, used to ploughing profits back, should ignore the need to cover his financial future and that of his dependants. Again, take professional advice.

Widows can be protected in one of three ways:

1. Part of the husband's pension can be given up at retirement in return for a pension continuing to the widow. Note that the decision to do this does not have to be made until retirement.
2. A widow's pension commencing at the husband's death before or after retirement can be bought separately out of the husband's tax-free contributions.
3. Life 'cover' usually ceasing at retirement can be bought, also separately as above.

Note that the effect of 2 and 3 above is to reduce the amount the husband can spend on his own pension: the *combined* premiums are subject to the overall maximum percentage of net relevant earnings.

Making a will

Anyone fortunate enough to own a house experiences a glow of satisfaction when reading of increases in the value of house prices. It is, however, a strange paradox that very few of us in this situation regard ourselves as persons of property. For those who are unwise enough not to make a will, this omission will be remedied by the Laws of Intestacy. These laws were based on a survey made of those who had made wills, and therefore it may be thought that the legislation does provide for the disposal of the estates of the majority. Yet, *your* estate represents *your* own property and it would not seem unreasonable that this should be disposed of after your death in the manner you desire.

We think everyone should forget any superstitious nonsense and make a will. We advise individuals not to use the ready-made printed forms which can be purchased from stationers. People making out home-made wills sometimes use ambiguous wording which can frustrate their true intentions, and cause considerable delay in settling the estate. We urge you to go to a solicitor. Charges for a straightforward will would not normally exceed £30. If you do not have a solicitor, your local Citizens' Advice Bureau can advise you, or you can write to the Law Society. You can also use the Trustee Department of your bank but it will still be necessary to consult a solicitor.

If you do not make a will, your estate will be distributed in accordance with the Laws of Intestacy. As an example, if you leave a wife or husband and children, then your wife or husband will receive:

(a) *To wife/husband*

The personal effects. £25,000 plus the income of half of the remainder for life, then the capital to your children.

(b) *To children*

Half of the remainder is held for your children who attain the age of 18 or marry earlier. If any of your children predecease you, leaving children, then his/her share is held for the benefit of his/her children who attain the age of 18 or marry earlier.

The important figure to note is the £25,000 quoted in (a) above. We referred to the glow you may have experienced when reading of increased house prices. If your home has shown a substantial appreciation then its value could well exceed the £25,000 which is transferred to the surviving spouse.

A widow could well be faced with financial difficulties and the prospect of having to sell the house. Failure to make a will can precipitate family squabbles and cause much unnecessary anxiety.

A wife needs a home that is hers. It must be truly hers — and that means legally. She will need sufficient income to maintain her standard of living and sufficient resources to fight the battle of inflation.

We strongly urge a husband to take the professional advice of his solicitor on the effects of Capital Transfer Tax (CTT). He can draw up your will to take advantage of the fact that CTT does not apply between husbands and wives subject only to UK domicile. There is a nil rate of CTT on the first £25,000 of the estate of the husband and the wife. The solicitor may well suggest that a husband provides a life interest to his wife if she survives him, an advance against capital to her, a gift of his property to his children after safeguarding the rights of his wife.

There are two scales for CTT. Table A is the scale for lifetime transfer and Table B is for transfers on death.

A	
Lifetime transfers	Rate %
0 - 25,000	Nil
25,000 - 30,000	5
30,000 - 35,000	7½
35,000 - 40,000	10
40,000 - 50,000	12½
50,000 - 60,000	15
60,000 - 70,000	17½
70,000 - 90,000	20
90,000 - 110,000	22½

B	
On death	Rate %
0 - 25,000	Nil
25,000 - 30,000	10
30,000 - 35,000	15
35,000 - 40,000	20
40,000 - 50,000	25
50,000 - 60,000	30
60,000 - 70,000	35
70,000 - 90,000	40
90,000 - 110,000	45

and so on.

If you made a will some time ago when Estate Duty was in force, then we suggest you check with your solicitor whether it would be wise to have the will revised. Generally speaking, wills should be reviewed at least every three years. Once your will has been made, changes can be effected simply and inexpensively by asking your solicitor to prepare a codicil, which is a kind of post-script to the will.

Arrange for your solicitor to keep the original of your will and let your bank keep a copy.

Points to remember

1. Before you retire, compare your estimated pre-retirement and post-retirement budgets so that you may plan effectively.
2. Make your savings work harder for you.
3. Keep an emergency reserve.
4. Make use of privileges offered to pensioners.
5. Make a will.

Chapter 5
Your Health

An essential ingredient

We have frequently been asked when one should start to prepare for retirement. As far as health is concerned, we would say 'the sooner the better!' All too often, health is something which people take for granted, only realising how precious it is when they lose it. One of the authors was talking recently to a group of employees nearing retirement. He asked which of the six aspects to be discussed they thought the most important. As usual, the majority said 'money'. However, one lady argued persuasively that good health was the most valuable asset a person can have in retirement. 'You may have all the money you need', she said, 'but you will be unable to get out and about to enjoy it if you lack good health.' She had suffered much illness in the past, was fighting her way back to good health, and spoke with the authority of her own experience. You may have enough capital to indulge your wish for a long and expensive cruise, but you will be disappointed if your body is in such poor shape that you are afraid to venture far from your doctor and home. Investment in financial terms means laying out money in the hope of future gain. We can all profit most by making a substantial investment in good health. 1978 was National Fitness Year, and much useful material has been published by specialist organisations such as the Health Education Council and the Sports Council.

The World Health Organisation has defined health as 'being in a state of complete physical, mental and social well-being'. It is not merely the absence of disease or infirmity. They were seeking a definition applicable to all age-groups, but it seems particularly apt for retired people.

This chapter deals with the basic questions of physical well-being: diet, exercise, health checks and warning signs. Yet it is significant that the World Health Organisation definition includes mental and social well-being. In earlier chapters we have emphasised the need for mental adjustment if you are to make the most of the new way of life that retirement brings, and to make the positive approach we urge upon all our readers. You also have to adjust to your new role in the social environment. After retirement, you still have a part to play in the community — perhaps it could even be a more active part, with the extra time available to you. We discuss this aspect in a following chapter.

Release from stress

In his book *Executive Ease and Disease*, Dr H Beric Wright, Deputy Chairman of the BUPA Medical Centre and Honorary Medical Adviser to the Institute of Directors, strongly emphasises the close relationship between stress and illness. When people are subjected to heavy stress, (and Dr Wright sees executives as being especially at risk) their bodies are likely to react. Defence mechanisms come into play. We have all met executives who cannot reach targets or produce results on time. They get headaches, or begin to suffer from insomnia, indigestion, or other illnesses, all of which can make life very miserable for them at the time.

So retirement can, on the one hand, bring positive benefits to health through the removal of stress associated with one's work. The slackening of pace and the greater opportunities for relaxation may bring quick relief from some of those ailments which have worried you from time to time at work.

On the other hand, there are negative aspects which can affect people who have not had the opportunity of preparing for the change from full-time work to retirement (or have closed their minds to the thought of it). Too often, we come across cases of people who conveniently forget that retirement will one day come to them personally, and when, inevitably, the day arrives they are subjected to a different kind of stress produced by fear of the future, loss of status and identity, and lack of purpose.

As people get older, they tend to resist change. Their attitudes are based on their past experience. They have got used to the routines which they have established over the years and they find it hard to break old habits. Thus, the mental approach to retirement is a vital factor as you enter this new phase of life. The way in which you plan and prepare ahead for the new experience can have a direct influence on your physical well-being in the future. If you think of life as a bottle, look on it as being still half full rather than already half empty!

The key-word

We offer a key-word for retired people when considering physical well-being: moderation.

The great majority of people are still vigorous and active when they retire, especially people in what doctors have called 'the robust 60s'. If you are one of these fortunate ones, you may find it difficult to accept the notion that you are no longer as young as you used to be. You may not yet be prepared to admit that at 60 plus it is no longer quite so easy to paper that wall, that climbing up that long ladder to clear the gutters is more hazardous, or that nipping across the High street dodging traffic, instead of waiting at the controlled crossing, is foolhardy! We could go on giving examples of ways in which people tend to overdo things and to take needless risks in an attempt to prove to themselves (though to nobody else) that they are still feeling young and active. An older person who carries this philosophy to extremes may become a menace to himself and a nuisance to others. So remember: moderation is the key-word.

As usual, there are two sides to the coin. In this instance, you should not look on retirement as a signal for a change to the common image of the poor old pensioner. In these days of competitive sport, we hear of swimming champions who are too old in their 20s, and professional boxers and footballers who are past their peak at the age of 30. This does not mean that at some arbitrary date, sportsmen and women are no longer any good at swimming, boxing, football or whatever their sport may be. They will go on enjoying their sport for a good many years to come. Similarly, retirement from work at some arbitrary date must not mean retirement from existing active leisure pursuits. We heard of one man in his 80s who still played tennis regularly. He enjoyed the game and it kept him fit and active. He had been playing tennis for very many years. However, it would be unwise for a 65-year-old pensioner to return to the squash court for a strenuous game after an absence from it of 15 or 20 years. Moderation has to be taken in the context of your own practice and experience.

The key-word applies to everything else we talk about in this chapter. In exercise, for instance, we have already pointed out the dangers facing the 'armchair and slippers brigade'. There is the other extreme: folk who hurl themselves into a frenzy of digging the garden, or decorating the house as soon as they retire, with the inevitable consequence of aching muscles and stiff backs, if nothing worse. Similarly, moderation in diet does not mean that you should become health food faddists. Our advice about seeing your doctor if your body starts to give you warning signs does not mean that you should spend your retirement contemplating a medicine cupboard full of so-called remedies for every imaginable illness.

Beware accidents

Now is the time, too, to look around your home and check that there are no loose ends of incomplete do-it-yourself jobs waiting to trap you into injury in an unwary moment. After all, you are certainly going to be around the home much more when you retire, so fix that faulty shelf now, and fasten down that loose rug or stair-carpet. There is no point in undertaking a programme of exercises if you trip over the carpet and end up with an arm or leg in plaster. Safety in the home is important and we will have more to say about it in chapter 8 on living arrangements, but remember: your health will also be dependent upon the avoidance of accidents.

Be comfortable

As people get older they tend to feel the cold more. Every winter there are sad tales of old and lonely people dying of hyperthermia. So never mind that youthful image; make sure you are warmly clad in the cold weather. Wear clothes for comfort even if they are not quite the latest thing in the fashion world. Also, it is no longer considered essential to have a bedroom window open all night, whatever the temperature outside. This is one Victorian idea we can safely dispense with. Breathing the cold and damp night air is not really good for your health. You sleep much better if you are warm and cosy in bed. But do bear in mind that as a general rule you need less sleep as you get older. If you allow yourself to spend most of the day dozing in your armchair, the chances are you will not sleep soundly the whole night through. It is far better to be active during the day, enjoying fresh air and exercise. That way you are more likely to sleep well at night, without having recourse to sleeping pills.

Smoking, drink and sex

We will take each of these items in turn. So far as smoking is concerned, if all the pronouncements by the Department of Health and other medical authorities have any weight at all, you must accept that smoking is a bad habit which adversely affects your health and is unpleasant for others near you who are non-smokers. There are degrees of smoking, like everything else, and probably one of the main reasons for excessive smoking is stress. You feel like throwing the telephone or typewriter out of the window in frustration, but instead you light another cigarette and fume away silently until you have calmed down. If you are trying to give up the habit now, don't let us delay you! If not, why not let retirement mark a special effort? After all, retirement means a release from the stresses of your job and a major change in your way of living, so it is the ideal opportunity. Succeed, and you will find a sharper sense of taste, enjoy the flavour of your food more, and improve your digestion. There is no need for us to emphasise the publicity given by the medical profession to the relationship between smoking and cancer, heart disease and chest troubles. It is enough to make everyone who cares about their health think seriously about stopping smoking. If stopping seems beyond you, at least cut down on cigarettes and don't inhale smoke into your lungs. Cigarette smokers who inhale the smoke find it very difficult to convert to non-inhaling, yet the inhalation of anything is the danger. Men might find it easier to change over to pipe smoking during the more leisurely days which retirement brings. That is thought to be less harmful. One of the authors who had tried several times to give up cigarettes, eventually changed to a pipe and later found it much easier to stop smoking altogether. There are many organisations which offer help and guidance on how to deal with the habit. Your local health education office or Citizens' Advice Bureau can provide you with useful literature, and possibly details of local courses designed to help smokers to get together to break the habit.

Drinking, in the sense of liquid intake, is something we all need — about six pints a day and it can be water, tea, coffee, fruit drinks and so on. When we think of drinking in respect of alcohol, we get back to our key-word: moderation. Of course it is wise to avoid alcohol altogether if your doctor considers it bad for your medical condition, or it will not mix with the pills he has prescribed for you. It is wise to ask your doctor, if you have any doubts on that score, also to consult him if you fear that drinking is becoming compulsive. Many people enjoy a glass or two at the 'local' from time to time, and one doctor we know swears that a good malt whisky at night is better than any sleeping pill for a sound night's rest!

The question of sexual needs seems to worry some couples as retirement looms, but there is no logical reason why sexual activity should not continue as normal. There is nothing abnormal in sexual activity among older people, and there is no deadline associated with retirement age so far as sexual desires and needs are concerned. Certainly these vary from one individual to another and are affected from time to time by such factors as stress and illness. If couples do find problems in their relationships as they get older, the family doctor can help and, if necessary, will refer them to an advisory clinic. Expert help and guidance are always available if you take the trouble to look for them.

Unwanted surplus

We heard one doctor tell a pre-retirement group that more people in the UK commit suicide with a knife and fork than any other weapon! He raised a few chuckles, but his main idea was to bring home to them the fact that the mortality rate for people who are 10 per cent overweight is 13 per cent higher than normal. It is far healthier to be slightly underweight than over. The middle-age spread is a common enough sight and most people accept it as normal and only to be expected. Yet it is neither natural, nor healthy. Nor is it inevitable.

We discuss exercise later in this chapter, but if you are overweight perhaps the first exercise is to push yourself away from the dining table! Food gives us energy, measured in terms of calories. If we do not use all that energy, the unused surplus is stored as fat. People who habitually consume more calories than they need gradually develop that chubby look. They have to start letting the tucks out, or loosening their belts. The process is so slow as to be almost imperceptible, yet when the weighing machine finally convinces them of the need for action they often expect to accomplish the reverse process in days rather than weeks and are discouraged if a special diet does not have immediate effect!

Eating is one of the enjoyments of life. Nowadays many people's idea of a good evening out consists of a leisurely wining and dining at a favourite restaurant. Apart from such special occasions, most people have established their eating habits by the time they reach middle-age, and have their special likes and dislikes. These factors — enjoyment, social custom and habit — often combine to encourage middle-aged people to eat as much, if not more, than they used to when they were much younger and far more active.

When retirement comes, with its more leisurely pace of living, lessening of stress and release from the rat-race, people tend to use even less energy than they did at work. They need fewer calories in order to maintain a steady weight. Yet few think of reducing their daily intake of food.

It would be foolish to suggest that everyone overweight will die earlier than those who are underweight. Statistically though, there is some truth in the saying: 'the longer the waistline, the shorter the life-line'! The following chart, reproduced by kind permission of The Health Education Council, is a guide to ideal weights for people aged 25 and over. Indoor clothing has been allowed for.

One very rotund gentleman, having studied the chart, concluded that he was not really overweight — he just needed to grow another six inches! This was taking wishful thinking to extremes!

The Weigh-In			

Height without shoes ft in	**Men** Small frame st lb st lb	Medium frame st lb st lb	Large frame st lb st lb
5 1	8 0 — 8 8	8 6 — 9 3	9 0 — 10 1
5 2	8 3 — 8 12	8 9 — 9 7	9 3 — 10 4
5 3	8 6 — 9 0	8 12 — 9 10	9 6 — 10 8
5 4	8 9 — 9 3	9 1 — 9 13	9 9 — 10 12
5 5	8 12 — 9 7	9 4 — 10 3	9 12 — 11 2
5 6	9 2 — 9 11	9 8 — 10 7	10 2 — 11 7
5 7	9 6 — 10 1	9 12 — 10 12	10 7 — 11 12
5 8	9 10 — 10 5	10 2 — 11 2	10 11 — 12 2
5 9	10 0 — 10 10	10 6 — 11 6	11 1 — 12 6
5 10	10 4 — 11 0	10 10 — 11 11	11 5 — 12 11
5 11	10 8 — 11 4	11 0 — 12 2	11 10 — 13 2
6 0	10 12 — 11 8	11 4 — 12 7	12 0 — 13 7
6 1	11 2 — 11 13	11 8 — 12 12	12 5 — 13 12
6 2	11 6 — 12 3	11 13 — 13 3	12 10 — 14 3
6 3	11 10 — 12 7	12 4 — 13 8	13 10 — 14 8
Women			
4 8	6 8 — 7 0	6 12 — 7 9	7 6 — 8 7
4 9	6 10 — 7 3	7 0 — 7 12	7 8 — 8 10
4 10	6 12 — 7 6	7 3 — 8 1	7 11 — 8 13
4 11	7 1 — 7 9	7 6 — 8 4	8 0 — 9 2
5 0	7 4 — 7 12	7 9 — 8 7	8 3 — 9 5
5 1	7 7 — 8 1	7 12 — 8 10	8 6 — 9 8
5 2	7 10 — 8 4	8 1 — 9 0	8 9 — 9 12
5 3	7 13 — 8 7	8 4 — 9 4	8 13 — 10 2
5 4	8 2 — 8 11	8 8 — 9 9	9 3 — 10 6
5 5	8 6 — 9 1	8 12 — 9 13	9 7 — 10 10
5 6	8 10 — 9 5	9 2 — 10 3	9 11 — 11 0
5 7	9 0 — 9 9	9 6 — 10 7	10 1 — 11 4
5 8	9 4 — 10 0	9 10 — 10 11	10 5 — 11 9
5 9	9 8 — 10 4	10 0 — 11 1	10 9 — 12 0
5 10	9 12 — 10 8	10 4 — 11 5	10 13 — 12 5

Diet

Hardly a week goes by without one or other of the popular
magazines or newspapers carrying an article about dieting and
suggesting some new method of losing weight. But if you do
want to lose weight, it is safest to proceed with caution and
moderation, so that the unwanted pounds and inches are lost
gradually. There is danger in eating too little when you have
the urge to slim. People who live alone are particularly
vulnerable in this respect. It is all too easy to resort to the
quick snack rather than go to the trouble of preparing a
cooked meal, and sometimes this tendency, coupled with a

determination to slim, results in an inadequate and unbalanced diet which does more harm than good. If you have a weight problem the wisest course is to consult your doctor and follow his expert advice.

The twentieth century has seen great changes in eating habits, particularly in developed industrial societies such as the UK. People eat less plant and cereal fibre, and far more sugar, fat and protein. Much of what we eat has been factory-processed, refined, or frozen. It arrives on the table complete with additives of various kinds. These are usually intended to improve colouring or taste, and to act as preservatives. Unrefined foods and fresh vegetables are still available. These usually require more chewing so that they have to be eaten more slowly and this, in turn, makes them more filling. They satisfy the appetite, yet give you fewer calories, which is all to the good.

Apart from the health hazards associated with being overweight, older people have a tendency to suffer from clogged arteries and high blood pressure. In recent years much has been written about levels of cholesterol in the blood. This is a substance which is present in everyone's blood, and its level is increased by some foods such as butter, cream, lard, bacon fat and other animal fats. An excessive level of cholesterol is a factor which increases the danger of blood clots. For this, among other reasons, we are advised to use polyunsaturated margarine and to cut down on our intake of dairy produce. Similarly, vegetable oils rather than animal fats are increasingly used for cooking. These measures are only necessary if there is a problem over cholesterol.

The main objective is to try and have a balanced diet which provides you with protein and includes fresh vegetables and fruit, raw as well as cooked. (The retired gardener may appreciate, even more, the benefits of investing in a greenhouse!).

Many dietitians extol the virtues of having a high fibre content in our diet, and consider it good sense to eat foods in their natural state, which our bodies are designed to assimilate. Such a diet includes wholemeal bread, cereals, porridge, fresh fruit and vegetables. Bran is particularly valuable. Retirement may give you a good opportunity to get away from the temptations of easily-prepared convenience foods of the packaged variety, and to get back to natural foods.

After all, you will have more time available for food preparation and cooking, and you could make incidental savings in the cost of housekeeping.

You can eat wisely and well without becoming a food fad, and it is worthwhile taking the trouble to make sure you do have a reasonably balanced diet, which could also involve your eating less and becoming more selective. Taking care with your diet is helpful to safeguard your health. Older people sometimes show signs of malnutrition and anaemia due to a lack of iron. An iron and vitamin supplement over the winter months is often helpful.

Exercise

If retired people are to maintain their physical well-being and mental alertness, they must ensure their bodies have sufficient exercise. This maxim applies to all ages, and not only to retired people, so the sooner you start the better. Far too many people in sedentary occupations avoid even the limited opportunities for exercise which present themselves. Instead they make every possible use of the material conveniences of our technological age. The short walk from house to garage and from the car park to the office is almost the daily limit. We have mentioned the danger of identifying too easily with the popular concept of 'retirement'. 'Exercise' is another word which invokes a mental picture. To many, it means a hard session of physical jerks: knees bend, stretch up, running on the spot, and so on, or perhaps indulging in a strenuous game of football, tennis or hockey. In fact, we can get much of the exercise we need in more ordinary and, to some, more enjoyable ways. A brisk walk, for instance, is in itself good exercise. If you are overweight and have decided to cut down on your input of calories, remember that you can also lose weight by increasing your output of energy. A brisk half-hour walk will burn up some 200 calories. Some pensioners we know find that having a dog as a pet not only gives them companionship but also an incentive for getting out to exercise themselves and the dog at the same time. If you move to a new area in retirement, walking a dog is an excellent way to meet other dog lovers. Cycling and swimming are both good ways of getting exercise. Others find that golf offers an absorbing interest, combining exercise and pleasure. The point of all these examples is to illustrate that you can exercise your muscles in many ways which are not associated with 'exercise' in its more formal sense. If you are still at work, try to get in a walk at lunchtime and, within reason, use the stairs instead of the lift. One executive proudly told us that he now made a point of walking up four flights of stairs to his office each day. (We became disillusioned when a member of his staff told us that the lift was out of order at the time!)

There is no doubt at all that moderate and regular exercise plays a large part in keeping you healthy. It keeps the muscles in trim, improves the circulation and helps to ward off illnesses such as heart disease and deterioration of the arteries. It is worth bearing in mind though, that the more informal types of exercise already discussed, whilst tremendously helpful in keeping the body in trim, do not always bring some of the lesser-used muscles into play. More deliberate forms of exercise are designed to tone up all parts of the body, and to increase strength and mobility. All muscles and joints have to be used if they are to continue to function properly.

As part of their 1978 Campaign, The Health Education Council produced a 'Look After Yourself' information pack, from which we have reproduced the following series of simple exercises. These exercise diagrams are reproduced by courtesy of The Health Education Council. The exercise schedule is devised by Al Murray, National and Olympic coaching adviser and Director of the City Gym Health Clinic.

For exercises 1 - 5, breathing should be free and easy, to fit the rhythm of the movement. About 10 or 12 repetitions is enough for each. For exercises 6 - 8, repeat 8 to 10 times and gradually increase to 20 or 30. Following the full routine will take only a few minutes. But if you can't face a daily exercise discipline, try it three times a week.

Before embarking on this programme or any other series of exercises, there are two things to be borne in mind. First, if you suffer from any physical disability, if you are already under treatment by your doctor, or if you have any doubts about your health, please consult your doctor beforehand. Secondly, remember that, like losing weight, getting physically fit is a gradual process and cannot be achieved in a few days. Sudden bursts of enthusiasm are likely to have the opposite effect to what you intend. You need to start gently. There is

1

ARM SWINGING
Start: Feet wide astride, arms hanging loosely by your sides.
Movement: Raise both arms forward, upwards, backwards and sideways, in a circular motion, brushing your ears with your arms as you go past.

2

SIDE BENDS
Start: Feet wide apart, hands on hips.
Movement: Bend first to the left and then to the right, keeping the head at right angles to the trunk.

3

TRUNK, KNEE AND HIP BENDS
Start: Stand 18" behind the back of a chair, with hands resting lightly on the back.
Movement: Raise the left knee and bring the forehead down to meet it. Repeat with the right knee. Do not rush. This must be a long, strong movement.
(NB. When you are used to this exercise, you can dispense with the chair and work from the standing position.

4

HEAD, ARMS AND TRUNK ROTATING
Start: Feet wide astride, hands and arms reaching directly forward at shoulder level.
Movement: Turn the head, arms and shoulder around to the left as far as you can go, bending the right arm across the chest, then repeat the movement to the right. Keep the hips and legs still throughout.

5

ALTERNATE ANKLE REACH
Start: Feet wide apart, both palms on the front of the upper left thigh.
Movement: Relax the trunk forward as you slide both hands down the front of the left leg. Return to upright position, then repeat on the right.
(NB. Those suffering from mild back trouble must not pass the knees with the hands.)

6

WALL PRESS-UPS
Stand with hands on wall 12″ apart at shoulder height, arms straight. Stand on your toes. then bend the arms until the chest and chin touch the wall. Return to start position by straightening arms.

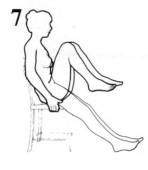

7

ABDOMINAL EXERCISE
This exercise will help flatten your tummy muscles. Sit on the front part of the chair, legs straight, heels on floor. Lean back and grip the sides of the seat for support. Bend the knees and bring the fronts of the thighs up to squeeze gently against the body. You can also do the same exercise with the legs held straight.

8

LEG EXERCISE
Stand 18″ behind a chair, with your hands on the back. Lower the body into a squat, keeping the feet flat on the floor (ladies may stand on their toes at this point). Straighten both legs and come up on the toes, then return to the squat position. You can dispense with the chair and place hands on hips.

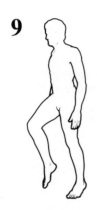

9

RUNNING ON THE SPOT
Stand with arms loosely by the sides and gently run on the spot. Do not begin by raising the knees high, but aim to get them higher as you progress. Start with a very short time — say 30 seconds, and gradually build up.

plenty of time to build up to a more ambitious programme later on.

Recent research into different forms of exercise as part of the remedial process following a heart attack has led some experts to believe that to be of benefit, exercise must have the effect of increasing the pulse rate significantly. It is unwise to let the pulse rate exceed 120 beats a minute and you can monitor it yourself with a little practice. (Count your pulse for 15 seconds and multiply the total by four). The jugular pulse in the neck is easier to count than the wrist pulse. But remember our warnings about consulting your doctor if you have any doubts. If, for example, you have heart trouble, your doctor may have prescribed pills which have the effect of reducing your pulse rate.

Books on physical exercise are usually available at the local library. For those who need the encouragement of working with others, many adult education colleges and institutes run courses, including yoga and medau, for adults of all ages.

Your invisible means of support

We are talking about your spine! Four out of five people suffer from back-ache at some time in their lives. Even before middle age, degenerative changes take place in the spine. Continuous wear and tear can have an insidious and unpleasant effect upon those discs of the spine. With the kind permission of the Back Pain Association, a registered medical charity, we have produced their Charter for back health, together with some of their diagrams:

HOW TO PREVENT BACK PAIN
Don't get overweight.
Avoid unnecessary heavy lifting.
If you must lift, use an approved technique (see diagrams).
Sit correctly, not round shouldered and slouching (see diagrams).
Choose a chair that gives firm support to your spine.
When sitting at work surfaces, make sure the height of your chair is right in relation to the working surface.
If possible, avoid spending long hours behind the wheel of a car.
If you can't avoid driving, make sure you've got a good car seat.

Arrange your work place or your kitchen so that you don't have to bend and stretch unnecessarily.

At all times, try to keep your back reasonably straight, and don't let your shoulders slump forward (see diagrams).

Buy yourself a really firm mattress, preferably a new one from a reputable firm.

Make sure you get a reasonable amount of exercise every day, but don't leap into violent and unaccustomed exercise!

Above all, remember: prevention is the *best* form of cure.

WORKING HEIGHTS

Don't stoop

Do make sure work-tops are the
    right height

DRIVING

Don't sit in a cramped position

Do use a back rest if the seat does
    not support the small of your back

SITTING

WRONG | RIGHT

Don't slouch or slump

Do choose chairs that support
the small of your back

LIFTING

WRONG | RIGHT

Don't bend your back

Do bend your knees and make your
legs do the heavy work

WALKING

WRONG | RIGHT

Don't slouch or hunch your shoulders

Do stand up straight

Back pain costs the nation over £300 million a year in terms of medical care, sickness benefit and lost production. The Back Pain Association is endeavouring to increase the amount of money spent on medical research on diseases of the back (at present only 7p in every £100). Ask the BPA for details of their literature if you are a back sufferer.

Some people, as they get older, are susceptible to aches and pains caused by arthritis and rheumatism. If you are a sufferer you can obtain literature from the British Rheumatism and Arthritis Association. This organisation has over 125 branches throughout the country.

Prevention better than cure

If you have a car, you will know that car manufacturers supply a handbook with each new vehicle. This gives advice on maintenance and servicing. Regular servicing according to the manufacturer's recommendations makes sense if you want trouble-free motoring. It is even more important to look after your health, and makes even more sense to have periodic health check-ups, say, once a year although there may apparently be nothing at all wrong with you. Periodic examinations by your doctor could lead to the early recognition of signs and symptoms which at that stage require only simple remedial treatment.

For instance, every year in the UK some 13,000 women die of cancer of the breast and nearly 2,500 die of cancer of the cervix. Early detection of these conditions gives the best chance of successful treatment, and for that reason regular breast and pelvic screening is a wise precaution for women, especially for those over 35 years of age. Critics of the National Health Service have suggested it should be re-named the National Sickness Service, because it concentrates too much of its efforts on curing disease rather than preventing it. Yet an increasing number of family practitioners are willing to give routine examinations, and you should have no hesitation in requesting one.

We have to accept that as we get older some of our senses begin to run down. Vision gradually deteriorates and for most of us, glasses become a necessity. But you can still preserve your eyesight by making sure that you always have a good light for reading or sewing. Make sure that you have your eyesight tested at regular intervals.

Regular visits to your dentist are also advisable if you are to keep a healthy mouth. Teeth require periodic checking, and dentures are liable to become ill-fitting after a few years.

For many people, hearing deteriorates after middle age, and a loss of hearing seems to evoke little sympathy from those more fortunate. You may yourself have felt irritated by another person's apparent stupidity and lack of understanding, although it was entirely owing to their being hard of hearing. Elderly people suffering from deafness, perhaps coupled with short-time memory, may become slightly paranoid — they cannot hear properly what is being said to them, and may come to believe that it is derogatory and unfriendly. This makes them suspicious of other people and, on occasions, determined to be awkward. It is a danger which should be recognised and guarded against. If you realise that you are becoming hard of hearing (and that it is not your friends who are speaking more softly), you would be wise to consult your doctor. There may be a simple remedy. Hearing aids are gradually becoming more socially acceptable. If the use of a hearing aid improves your hearing it is surely wise to use one!

Regular visits to the chiropodist are also worthwhile if you have any sort of foot trouble. Even in this age of mechanised transport, by the time you are 60 your feet will have carried you many thousands of miles and might deserve some expert attention.

If you have difficulty in remembering when the time has arrived for you to make the arrangements for routine examinations by the doctor, dentist, optician, or chiropodist, why not link the whole lot to one date such as your birthday. Then when that day comes around each year it will remind you that it is time to make appointments for your annual health checks. The collection of your retirement pension book also means that you hold the passport to some medical services at reduced rates, or even free of charge. Consult your local Age Concern office.

An effective way of obtaining a thorough and comprehensive health testing, is through the BUPA Medical Centres in London or Manchester. 1,000 patients a month go through the health testing programme at the London Centre. Tests include x-rays of chest and abdomen, electro-cardiograph

and blood pressure, height, weight and skinfold thickness, lung
function tests, hearing and vision, urine tests, an automated
medical history, and some 20 other assorted tests which look
for diseases of the liver, kidneys or blood, diabetes, signs of
heart disease and other conditions. There is also a separate
unit which carries out screening for women. Patients attend
the Centre from all over the world. Although there are special
reduced fees for BUPA subscribers and members of the
Institute of Directors, anyone may use the Centre. Patients
have to have their own doctor's consent to go for a check-up,
and afterwards their doctor receives a full report.

Warning signs

There is no longer any need for people to take aches and
pains for granted, as a sign of advancing years. Your body
often gives you an early warning that something is amiss.
When that happens it is wise to see your doctor without
delay. Early diagnosis of a disease can often bring quick
and effective treatment. Ignoring the body's warnings or
trying to put up with discomfort in the hope that it will go
away may lead to more prolonged and serious trouble later
on. For instance, older men are sometimes liable to suffer
from enlargement of the prostate gland. This causes difficulty
in emptying the bladder, and in the end severe discomfort.
Yet the condition can be treated by a relatively simple and
safe operation which should be carried out earlier rather than
later, if more serious problems are to be avoided. The
following are the main sort of warning signs which call for
attention:

1. A pain which lasts for more than a few days.
2. An unexplained swelling, even though it may not be
   painful at first.
3. A persistent cough or hoarseness.
4. Unusual bleeding from any part of the body.
5. Dizziness, shortness of breath, chest pain or
   palpitations.
6. Constipation, indigestion and changes in bowel habits.
7. Persistent tiredness and headaches or migraine.
8. Unexplained loss of weight or changes in skin condition.
9. Sleeplessness and depression.

To contemplate such a list for any length of time would be enough to drive a hypochondriac to despair, so do not brood over it. The point is that if at some time in the future you recognise one of these symptoms, you know that you should consult your doctor about it. But they are far less likely to arise at all if you take positive steps to protect your health in the ways we have suggested. Try, if you can, to establish a friendly relationship with your doctor. If he is called out suddenly to your home in some emergency, it is helpful if he knows you as a person rather than a name on an index card. When your insurance company demands a medical examination before your car insurance is renewed, you will have to see him anyway.(Note that you will have to pay for such a medical.) Life will be easier if your doctor has seen you regularly and knows your history.

Points to remember

1. Good health in retirement is dependent upon three crucial factors: physical, mental and social well-being.
2. Retirement brings release from stresses arising from work and can have a resulting beneficial influence on physical well-being.
3. Moderation in all things should be the key-word. People of retirement age should accept that they are no longer at the peak of their physical prowess. But retirement should not be the signal to give up existing active pursuits.
4. Care must be taken to avoid accidents. Possible hazards around the house should be eliminated and the house made comfortable and warm in winter.
5. Being overweight is a health risk. It is prudent to keep weight down to the recommended level, but never to attempt crash slimming diets. Doctors will advise on weight problems and dieting. A balanced diet is important.
6. Exercise is essential to maintain physical well-being and mental alertness. Physical exercise can be taken in many enjoyable ways and not merely through formal exercise sessions.
7. Periodical health checks with doctor, dentist, optician and chiropodist are advisable. If the body starts to give warning signs that something is amiss, the doctor should be consulted immediately. Delay could mean more prolonged treatment later on.

Chapter 6

It's Leisure Time

Laws of demand and supply

During our working lives, we place a high value on our precious leisure hours, which are the times when we can put work out of our minds for a little while and please ourselves as to what we choose to do. It may be taking an active part in a favourite sport, or watching it; devoting time to a special hobby; looking at television; or simply enjoying the everyday pleasures of family life or companionship with others. When heavy pressures of work are so demanding that we have to give up much of our leisure time, we eventually reach a stage in which we attach even more importance to those spare-time pursuits we are having to forego. We feel particularly disappointed about having to give up that weekend game of golf; to skip the next meeting of our local society; or to miss the latest episode of the current TV serial. In fact, we heartily endorse the sentiment that leisure is more valuable when it is in short supply! Unlike our working hours, our leisure time is not committed to our employer, so in this sense only we can organise it and give it direction and purpose.

One personnel officer of our acquaintance makes a point of asking all prospective trainees what they do in their spare time. He is no longer surprised at the number who find it difficult to mention even one positive and active interest. He also talks to older employees as they approach retirement age. Sadly, some of these also have no special leisure-time interests, and have no plans for doing anything in particular when they have retired from work.

Yet statistically, the average man or woman retiring from full-time employment today has an additional 2,000 hours a year leisure time available. Imagine yourself waking up on the first morning of your retirement. The alarm clock has been left off and you lie in bed with a feeling of well-being and tranquillity. At last retirement has arrived and your time is your own. You think what a wonderful thing retirement is. But, having reached it at last, what are you going to do with it?

Many people find it difficult to think of leisure other than in the purely negative concept of 'time free from work' or 'spare time'. The work-orientated society in which we live conditions us to this view. When retirement comes, this obvious distinction between work and leisure is lost. At that stage in life it is better to get away from the measurement of leisure purely in terms of time to be spent, and rather to look at it as a combination of interests and activities. These are related to time, but only in the sense that it has to be allocated between those various leisure interests and activities.

Planning (although easier said than done) is an essential part of preparation for retirement. It is a time for broadening horizons, expanding current interests and discovering fresh fields to conquer. A negative approach, leading to a loss of interest in what is happening around you and a gradual withdrawal from activity and personal relationships, brings in its train only loneliness and isolation. These are not the ingredients for a happy retirement. Make your planning positive and purposeful, if you are determined to enjoy your retirement to the full.

Of course, you may have an answer straight away. Perhaps you already have plans for making full use of your leisure hours. If so, you are to be congratulated! During their time with the Pre-Retirement Association, the authors had the pleasure of meeting any number of people in their 70s and 80s who were thoroughly enjoying their lives and were delightful to talk to. Many were bubbling with enthusiasm. So far as they were concerned, it was not merely a question of taking up a hobby in their retirement, as a means of finding something to do in their 'spare time'. For them, there was no such thing as 'spare time'. They wished they could have more hours in the day so that they could devote more time to the various activities which absorbed their energies and interest. If the contents of *your* retirement programme include a wide variety of interesting activities you should be well equipped for a happy retirement.

Some people look forward to retirement with the idea that it will give them an opportunity to expand a relaxing spare-time hobby into an absorbing interest. But this does not always work out in practice. To many of these people, their hobby represents a pleasant diversion from the pressures of work and a satisfying way of achieving happy relaxation. But can that spare-time hobby give them full satisfaction in retirement? Professor Parkinson developed a theory that people expand their work to fill the time available. This is clearly demonstrated in numerous work situations. We very much doubt whether the theory would apply to a hobby in retirement, unless it is a really absorbing interest! There may be physical or financial limitations. It would be unwise to expect that one could spend *all* one's time in the garden in all seasons after retirement, even though, before retirement, it may provide a pleasant means of relaxation outside working hours. Similarly, not *all* amateur photographers using colour film could afford the cost of expanding their hobby into a full-time interest. There is a danger too, that the one-track person may find that not everyone shares his or her enthusiasm in the chosen hobby. We believe that the majority of people find greater satisfaction through a variety of interests which, combined, leave them with no 'spare time' at all.

Variety is the spice of life

We have heard many lecturers on the subject of retirement talk about people having time on their hands, and how that time should be used. We know of one course organiser who invariably arranged a special session in each of his courses, devoted to a talk by a gardening expert. The expert was a very good speaker, and all those attending the course found the talk fascinating if they happened to be interested in gardening as a hobby. The others either found the talk boring, or snoozed quietly at the back of the room until the talk was over. This was particularly likely if the gardening session immediately followed the lunch hour! Luckily, most of us vary widely in our interests, and are a mixture which defies such treatment. There is no easy way of classifying hobbies and interests into arbitrary categories, designed to suit groupings of people according to their individual characteristics.

How then, are we to advise a person nearing retirement, who has no particular spare-time interests, but who realises that there is value in taking up one or more on retirement?

There are several guidelines which are worth considering:

1. CURRENT INTERESTS

In a special notebook, briefly jot down at the end of each day, for the next few weeks, how you have occupied your leisure time. (You may also be interested in noting the number of hours spent each day at work and in travelling to it and back again. The total should be impressive after a few weeks!) Some items will crop up regularly in your daily jottings, but whatever time you spend on actually *doing* something, note it down. As time goes on you could well be surprised at the time you have logged up in eating, watching television, or even in doing nothing much at all! When you have analysed the results of this project, you may have some regrets that you have wasted so much time in doing nothing in particular. Or the record might show you how you could usefully adjust the spare time available to you so as to make a more purposeful allocation of it to one of your special interests. The project will at least help you to make a short list of the activities which have taken up a significant proportion of your leisure hours. Are they hobbies and interests which you really enjoy and which you would like to develop further when you have time available? On the other hand you may decide, on reflection, that there are some activities which are not worth spending so much time on in future. Perhaps the project will prove to be so fascinating in itself that you will have found a new interest in continuing such a daily record. If, when you have compiled your list of activities it is so brief that it seems hardly worth the trouble of making it, at least take it as a warning signal that you need to give some thought to the question of what you will do with your time in retirement.

2. AT SCHOOL AND WORK

Here is another exercise for you. Make a list of the subjects which you used to like or were good at when you were at

school. (Usually children are good at the subjects they
particularly enjoy.) Then add to the list any other aspects of
school life which you enjoyed, apart from the lesson times.
Can you add a note of other activities or subjects that you
wanted to take at school, but missed the opportunity to do so
for one reason or another? What subject were you best at and
which was your special favourite? Would it be worthwhile
pursuing further studies in those subjects, now that you have
more time available?

What of work? Some fortunate people leave school or
college to take up a job which offers them a direct opportunity
to develop their particular abilities and special interests. Others
find themselves in jobs in which they eventually develop latent
abilities, unrealised at school — for example in salesmanship,
analysis and classification, or journalism.

Think about your work for a moment, and decide which
aspect of it has given you the most satisfaction. What aspects
of it do you dislike? What special skills or professional
knowledge have you been able to develop?

By reviewing the experiences of your school days and later
your working life you should be able to pinpoint those things
which you have enjoyed doing, the things you have been
specially good at, and the things which have given you little
or no pleasure at all.

3. FRUSTRATED AMBITIONS

In the previous paragraph we mentioned the fortunate ones
who find themselves in the right niche when they leave school
or college. Many young people, however, find themselves a
job and (almost by accident) start a life-time's career in some
specialised sphere of work. This probably applied to the
majority of young people who started work in the 1930s, when
the level of unemployment was high and jobs were hard to get.
Perhaps there was an opening in father's office, or a family
friend knew of a vacancy. For someone offered an
appointment in a large organisation, much could depend
upon the particular section or department to which he or she
was allocated. If your career was determined by chance in that
way, perhaps there is something which you have always
dreamed of doing, but never had the opportunity to do, either
at school, at work, or in the limited amount of leisure time
you have had available.

We heard of one young man who left school in the early 1930s and whose father, a chartered accountant, was determined his son should never be unemployed. He judged that if his son also qualified as a chartered accountant this would be a passport to a secure career. The son was dragooned into taking articles, and in due course obtained his qualification. The father overlooked the fact that his son really had no great love for figures. Had his son been completing his education today he would have chosen to have become an archaeologist. The son remained in the accountancy profession, but all his spare time was devoted to archaeology. His holidays were spent visiting ruins in Turkey and Greece, and assisting with archaeological 'digs'. The son retired recently, having gladly taken the opportunity for early retirement. Now, with his wife, he spends much of his time in the Mediterranean region. You have probably guessed his part-time occupation! He joins the tourist ships cruising round the Greek Islands and escorts speciality tours devoted to visits to the ruins. We hear that this would-be archaeologist is rejuvenated; his 'retirement' is giving him the satisfaction and enjoyment which he never obtained from his career.

Of course, some frustrated ambitions are no longer realisable when you reach retirement age. The boyhood dream of becoming a racing driver, or the schoolgirl hopes of becoming a ballerina, must remain a part of childhood fantasy, and none of us is likely to compete in the next Olympics, no matter how keen we once were in the field of athletics and sport.

Nevertheless, make a note now of any of the things you always wished you could do if you had the chance, and which could still be practical if you really put your mind to it.

4. COMPLETING THE PICTURE

To complete the exercise, the next step is to compare the various lists you have so conscientiously compiled — your current leisure interests, the things you used to enjoy doing at school, the aspects of your work which have given you most satisfaction, and the things which you always wanted to do if you had the opportunity. What does the comparison show? You should be able to put your preferred activities into broad categories. Do they come under one or more of the following headings?

1. Artistic and creative interests (eg music, painting, embroidery, photography).
2. Practical interests (eg do-it-yourself work in the home, repair work, gardening).
3. Physical interests (eg swimming, golf, bowls, cycling, jogging, yoga).
4. Intellectual interests (eg studying and searching for further knowledge on chosen subjects).
5. Community interests (eg local government, voluntary work in helping handicapped or deprived people, counselling and advisory work).
6. Social interests (eg membership of clubs or associations, meeting and talking to other people).
7. Organisational interests (eg committee and secretarial work, accounting and administration).
8. Literary interests (eg reading, writing articles and letters, poetry).
9. Political or religious interests (eg canvassing support, church activities).

You may be able to improve upon our list of categories and to add additional ones of your own. You soon come to realise that most activities involve more than one of these classifications. For instance, the few examples given in class 1 (artistic and creative interests) could also involve classes 2, 4 and 6. Class 5 could also involve classes 6 and 7, and so on.

Some interests are primarily restricted to one particular classification, but could be extended into other categories according to individual preference. For instance, swimming is fairly and squarely within class 3. It is a physical activity and it can be enjoyed without involving other people at all. But if a competent and keen swimmer is also of a social bent (class 6) he or she could join a swimming club and so find companionship and social contacts. There might also be an opportunity to coach schoolchildren for life-saving certificates. If our swimmer is also a good organiser and administrator (class 7) he or she might fill a need in the club for an honorary secretary or treasurer, or a competitions organiser. We might take this example a further stage. Some swimmers are interested in the therapeutic value of swimming, particularly in the case of some muscular disabilities.

A swimmer interested in voluntary work (class 5) might find scope for such help at a special hospital unit. In this instance, the retired person would be allocating part of the time to an enjoyable leisure pursuit, would be fulfilling a useful purpose and so gaining personal satisfaction, and would be making new friends and social contacts to replace those lost on leaving work.

We have given just a few examples to show ways in which your own interests, abilities, skills and knowledge might be linked to bring you greater satisfaction and enjoyment in the use of your leisure hours. We hope that by following the exercises we have described you will have gained a better idea of the types of activities which are likely to give you enjoyment. In that case, you may already have a sound notion of what you propose to do with all that new-found leisure time. If so, how are you to obtain the greatest satisfaction from your chosen interests? If not, how can you set about discovering new and satisfying interests which will fill the bill, so far as you have been able to classify your preferences? There are several sources from which you might get the information (or inspiration) you need.

(a) *The public library*
Many people simply regard the local library as the place to go when they want a light novel, or a detective story, to while away a few idle hours. There is usually a crowd around the fiction shelves. Yet nearly all public libraries maintain a large non-fiction and reference section, in which you can find books on a wide variety of subjects which may prove a treasure house of ideas and information. A browse around these shelves would probably spark off some new interest, or remind you that perhaps you still have more to learn about a subject which already gives you enjoyment in your leisure hours. There is usually an experienced and qualified librarian available to give you any help or guidance you require.

Let us give you another example. A pensioner we know came across an article in the library about treasure hunting with a metal detector. The librarian obtained further information on the subject and now our pensioner friend is so keen that he studies maps of battles fought in bygone years. His hobby takes him off the beaten track (where his detector is less likely to locate discarded metal bottle tops), and he enjoys the exercise in the open air, although he takes care not to offend against the wishes and requirements of those whose task it is to protect our national heritage.

(b) *Adult education*

The old concept that evening classes are primarily intended for young people learning typing, shorthand, book-keeping, or kindred subjects related to their jobs, is out of date. Local education authorities have long been aware of the fact that education is not solely the prerogative of young people, and that there is an ever-growing demand, from people of all ages, for educational facilities in the broadest sense of the term. There are older people whose educational experience is restricted to the formal tuition of their schooldays, who are afraid that they will feel embarrassed when presenting themselves at some course or other at the local institute of adult education. Their fears are unfounded. Unless you live in the depths of the countryside, you are likely to be within reasonable distance of a centre of adult education, offering courses on a wide variety of interesting subjects. People of all ages attend these courses, many of which are designed for beginners. Classes are conducted in an informal and friendly manner, and in most areas the already modest charges are still further reduced for people of retirement age. If you live in a large town or city you will find that the adult education movement offers a range of activities during the day-time as well as in the evening. In many areas the Workers' Educational Association runs interesting day-time courses. In large towns there are now liberal arts colleges set up by the education authority which provide day-time and evening courses covering a wide range of leisure activities in the fields of art, music and drama. Your local library will be able to give you details of all courses available in your area.

Then there are residential colleges which run specialised courses of all types, ranging in length from a weekend to a week or more. These colleges are usually situated in delightful surroundings, and students can enjoy the amenities in a relaxed atmosphere in company with other people who have similar interests. Residential courses are also provided by Field Study centres, which run courses devoted to various aspects of natural history. The National Institute of Adult Education publishes details of forthcoming residential courses, every six months. (See Useful Addresses for address.)

Many of the universities run extra-mural classes, some of which are residential. These are generally concerned with subjects to be studied in the university itself.

For those with the determination to learn more about their chosen subject, the Open University provides a wonderful opportunity to obtain a university degree irrespective of age or previous educational attainments. Many retired people are taking Open University courses and several can already boast of their achievement in obtaining a degree. You can study in your home, at your own pace, refer problems to a tutor living in your area, and meet fellow students at tutorials or summer schools. Full information can be obtained from the Information Services department of the University. (See Useful Addresses for address.)

(c) *Local associations*
Some years ago, one of the authors was closely involved in the preparation and publication of a Borough Guide. The most time-consuming part of the project was the compilation of what seemed at the time to be an almost endless list of local clubs and associations, covering nearly every aspect of the life of the community. These ranged from youth organisations such as Boy Scouts, Girl Guides, Sea Rangers, Covenanters and so on, to ex-service associations, sports clubs of various kinds, Women's Institutes and Townswomen's Guilds, Rotary and Round Table clubs, camera clubs, rambling clubs, social clubs, Darby and Joan clubs, etc etc, until there were some six or more closely printed pages of names, addresses and telephone numbers. Keeping such a list up to date is a continual headache for the information staff at the town hall or Council offices, but you will find it well worthwhile to enquire. You may find that there is a local organisation devoted to your particular hobby or interest.

We hope that this chapter on leisure has helped you to crystallise your thoughts, and perhaps given you some insight into the great number of opportunities available to you in expanding existing interests, and discovering new ones. The important thing to remember is that, in retirement, you are in sole command: it is for you to decide what to do with all the leisure time available. When you have decided upon the various activities which you think will provide you with an interest, find out all you can about them and make up your mind to have a go. Make a start even if you feel diffident about it at first. Once you are over the first hurdle, you could be on the way to becoming an expert in an absorbing interest. Retirement brings new opportunities and opens up fresh possibilities for enjoyment and perhaps service to others, which we deal with in the next chapter.

Now is the time to explore new interests and, as the Council of Europe Working Party puts it: 'to preserve creativity and curiosity, the ability to marvel, and the capacity to listen and learn'.

Activities

Here is a list of 100 of the more popular hobbies and interests which appeal to people in retirement.

Amateur dramatics (acting, directing, make-up, set designing, stage management)
Amateur radio (transmitting and receiving)
Antiques
Archaeology
Archery
Art (appreciation, drawing, painting, designing, sculpture, wood carving)
Astronomy

Basketry
Beekeeping
Bell-ringing (campanology)
Billiards/snooker
Bird-watching
Bookbinding
Bowls
Brass rubbing
Bridge

Calligraphy
Camping
Caravanning
Car maintenance, repair and restoration
Chess
China restoration and decorating
Church work
Clock and watch repairing
Coin collecting

Conjuring
Cookery (continental, *haute cuisine*, patisserie, vegetarian, etc)
Cricket (scoring for local club)
Crochet
Croquet
Crossword puzzles
Cycling

Dancing (old time, folk, country, ballroom)
Darts
Debating
Do-it-yourself home repairs and decorating
Dressmaking

Ecology and conservation
Embroidery
Enamelling
Engraving

First aid
Fishing
Flower arranging
Foreign languages
Furniture making, repair, renovating

Gardening
Genealogy
Geology

Glass decorating and
  engraving
Golf

Heraldry
Homemade wine, beer, preserves
Hospital radio

Interior designing

Jewellery making
Jigsaw puzzles

Keep fit
Kite-making and flying
Knitting

Lace-making
Lacquer work
Leather work
Lecturing

Marquetry
Metal work
Millinery
Model-making
Motorboat cruising
Music (appreciation, playing an
  instrument, instrument making
  and repair, tape recording,
  choral singing and opera,
  orchestral/band playing)

Open University degree course

Pets (keeping and/or breeding
  dogs, cats, fish, birds)
Photography
Picture-framing
Politics (central/local government)

Pottery
Printing
Public speaking
Puppetry

Rambling
Reading
Rug-making

Sailing
Scrapbook making
Stamp collecting
Swimming

Table tennis
Tailoring
Tapestry work
Tennis
Toy making
Translating

Upholstery

Voluntary work with local
  associations (counselling,
  advising, administrating)

Walking
Weaving
Woodwork
Writing (articles, books, poetry)

Yoga

Zoology

Points to remember

1. Retirement makes another 2,000 hours a year available for leisure. The distinction between work and leisure is lost.
2. It is wise to have a variety of interests for retirement, rather than trying to expand one part-time hobby into a full-time interest.
3. People who have no special leisure interests on retirement may find new opportunities by analysing present spare-time activities, aspects of school and working life which have appealed in the past, and former ambitions still capable of achievement.

4. Possibilities can be looked at in broad categories and preferences considered.
5. Useful sources of information and further opportunities may be found through the local library, adult education courses and local clubs and associations.

Chapter 7

Paid Employment and Voluntary Work

Working for love or for money

Shakespeare had a more elegant phrase: 'If all the year were playing holidays, to sport would be as tedious as to work' *(Henry IV, part I).* In chapter 4 we suggested that you should attempt to gauge your retirement income. The result of that exercise should show whether you will need to look for part-time paid work in retirement in order to maintain the lifestyle to which you have grown accustomed during your working life. You may also feel that it might be easier and less stressful to work rather than to make restricting economies in your spending. On the other hand, if your budget just about balances you may feel able to offer your services to a voluntary cause, provided your out-of-pocket expenses can be met: or you may be able to help a charity or a voluntary body without return.

Must I seek work of any kind, you may ask? Certainly there must be time to 'stand and stare' but in 1974 a conference organised by the Centre International de Gérontologie Sociale spent five days debating 'Preparation for Retirement and the Quality of Life'. The objectives of the course included the following statement:

'In our continually changing society, it is essential to consider the life of the retired worker today in a new light. Indeed, the problem of adaptation of the individual to inactivity is most often accompanied by psychological and physiological disorders.'

Work in some shape or form is the finest antidote to combat the problem which complete inactivity will create after a life-long routine of work. Work, in fact, is a link with life.

Apart from financial considerations, many people find that

exclusion from their previous office means they miss the teamwork and the companionship of their former colleagues. For the 'workaholic' who is one hundred per cent wrapped up in his work, some type of occupation is a therapeutic necessity, for he is hard hit when his company bids him fond farewell. His conviction that he was indispensable makes him specially vulnerable to the unexpected shock which retirement can bring. Some years ago, in the House of Lords, Lord Raglan, who was then the President of the Pre-Retirement Association, drew attention to the iniquitous effect of the earnings rule, which was then far more severe. He suggested that a figure should be produced of what it costs the Health Service to deal with the psychosomatic ailments of the older age groups, who are discouraged from working, when the whole of their upbringing, education and training has taught them to need a job, to be useful, to be wanted. As Thomas Carlyle said: 'Work is the grand cure of all the maladies and miseries that ever beset mankind'. Yet it is increasingly difficult for older people to find this kind of employment. The high unemployment figures are likely to remain for some years, and many people believe that employment for younger people should take priority over the needs of the older ones.

However, as with other aspects of retirement preparation, long-term planning will increase your opportunities of acquiring additional income from earnings. Assess realistically your own abilities. After all, you have a wealth of experience. List your particular interests, and areas of special knowledge. Do not let your previous career act as a veil to prevent your seeing new openings. A new occupation can be a tremendous stimulus. Some members of the teaching profession go to pieces when they have left the classroom, yet one retired headmaster we have the privilege of counting amongst our friends has a sparkling extrovert personality. Now well into his 70s, he lectures regularly in retirement courses and, without a single note, never fails to captivate his audience. He acts as a leisure consultant to a leading travel company, writes plays, books, poetry, talks to Rotary presidents on the art of public speaking, and cheerfully offers his services free to aspiring authors. He has never been busier or happier, and his face reflects that inner warmth. He does not have time to wonder if he has lost status since he retired. His motto is: 'It is not what you retire from that counts, but what you retire *to*.'

Look forward, then, and decide what you will be happiest doing. Dealing with people or paper? Handling machinery? Driving a car?

Many people in retirement spend fruitless hours writing letters of application for various posts. The only result is a heavy postage and stationery bill. To strangers who do not know you, your age may count against you. G Watkin Williams was formerly Director of the Retirement Advisory Bureau run by the Institute of Directors. Another sprightly 70-year-old, his advice to persons approaching retirement and needing further employment is, 'to circulate and to communicate'. Your colleagues, your friends, your fellow club members, Rotarians, or Women's Institute members are the people who know you and recognise your qualities. Let your friends know well in advance the date of your retirement and tell them that you will then be looking for x hours of work a week as an accountant, secretary, school meals supervisor, lecturer or whatever you think is your *métier.* (It may well be something quite different from the job from which you have retired.)

You can use the Department of Employment's facilities to help find a second career, but the older you are the less enthusiastic will be the reception they offer you. This is, rightly or wrongly, a youth-orientated society and the young unemployed are more vociferous than their senior colleagues. Read the little cards in local shop windows, for you will not wish in retirement to travel long distances to work. We like the story of the retired solicitor who, bored with retirement, noticed that an advertisement for an office junior remained in a local shop window for some weeks. He answered the advertisement somewhat hesitantly. He did not reveal his legal background, but merely stated he had had a high school education. The desperate office manager took him on. He now works every afternoon; he is in charge of the postal franking and office duplicating services, and he has completely reorganised the filing system. The office staff turn to him for fatherly advice, and his wife says: 'he looks years younger!'

Ask your local Citizens' Advice Bureau if there is an employment agency for senior citizens in your area. Some retirement associations help in this way. For example, the Glasgow Retirement Council successfully operates a Part-time Employment Bureau for the retired. In spite of the high unemployment figures in Glasgow, the Bureau, staffed entirely by volunteers, all of them pensioners, has found an average of 200 jobs a year for retired people.

There are specialised agencies to help the older job-seeker. The experience and success of these agencies in placing clients has led them to analyse the comments received from employers. Companies which have employed older people report that they have found these workers show loyalty, punctuality, reliability, versatility and 'a willingness to do a full day's work'. Many more men than women in the 60-plus age group seek work — no doubt influenced by the differences in the state's arbitrary retirement ages. The agency Success after Sixty stated that 70 per cent of males seeking their help were in the age group 60 - 69. Most of the job-seekers said they needed work to increase income, though nearly as many said that they wanted work in order to avoid boredom and frustration. By continuing on a part-time basis this enables them to use their knowledge, keep their minds active, and continue to be useful and wanted members of the community.

Employers are becoming increasingly receptive to the idea of employing older people on a part-time basis, but you must be prepared to persevere. Choice of district for your retirement home is pertinent. London and other large cities offer more jobs and in greater variety than the small towns where the demand may be less. Perseverance, with a realistic strategy without undue heed to status, will bring results.

Kay Sykes was formerly Staff Officer for London Weekend Television. When she retired from that company she became Managing Director of Part-time Careers Ltd. Although this agency deals with all age groups, Mrs Sykes found that many of her clients came from the older age groups and she has had a success rate of 37 per cent in placing secretaries in the over-60 age bracket. Part-time Careers emphasise that their aim is to place all age groups in *permanent* part-time office jobs rather than in temporary work. Also, the agency's experience is that many women these days want to be more financially independent.

The financial contribution that women can make nowadays is often essential to balance the family budget. Where husbands have been made redundant, or obliged to take early retirement, the capacity of married partners to switch the roles of breadwinner has often saved the situation. Mrs Sykes found, in conducting interviews with women over 35, that the main obstacle to their getting a job was managing to obtain an actual interview with a prospective employer. Once this hurdle was cleared, it was probable that the candidate would be successful. Many employers are getting used to the fact that the older and perhaps more tolerant woman can have a stabilising effect in an office; that personality and experience count more than age. (This applies equally to the older man.) There is work available for statisticians, receptionists, librarians, analysts, in market development and in research, apart from the more obvious secretarial and clerical fields.

Yet the older woman should avoid trying to take on too much. If she does return to paid work, her husband should take over some of the household duties. Women who attempt too much can become over-tired, depressed and irritable. Men too!

Remember that there are opportunities for women whose secretarial skills may be rusty to take a refresher course. Check with the Department of Employment concerning the Training Opportunities Scheme (TOPS), or with the local education authority. You may then decide to take a training course in a new skill which will open up new possibilities.

The Employment Fellowship

The Employment Fellowship is a charitable organisation set up to encourage the foundation and maintenance of workshops for retired people. Its object is to support activity in retirement.

It runs Employment Fellowship centres which offer activities to the retired and elderly, who may otherwise suffer from boredom and the loss of companionship. The Fellowship realises that if it can harness the skills which many elderly people have, it can help them to maintain their independence, and consequently their dignity.

Work centres execute work on a sub-contract basis, much of if of a light industrial nature, often relieving bottlenecks in highly automated production plants.

The Fellowship often acts in a consultant capacity to local authorities and development corporations in increasing resources for care-schemes for the elderly.

Anyone with an engineering or administrative background who believes that activity in retirement will keep him fitter for a longer time, and who would like to help, should write to the Employment Fellowship's energetic and enterprising Director, Tom Oakman.

FELLOWSHIP EMPLOYMENT BUREAUX (BURETIRE)

The experience of the Employment Fellowship in setting up Work Centres proved that very little was being done for those unskilled in supervising workshops but who nevertheless wanted to work in industry or commerce. To supplement existing voluntary organisations, the Fellowship has created an organisation known as Buretire to cope with the increasing needs of people in early retirement for part-time employment. In 1975, a pilot employment bureau was established in a London borough. Originally intended to be non-profit-making, it now operates on a sound basis of profitability, and receives its income from placement fees. Other branches have been set up, and a special project has been launched with one of the Rotary districts.

Buretire has succeeded in providing employment for people which is suitable to both their experience and their personal inclinations. Examples of placements made include:

(a) Retired civil servant placed with an investigation bureau.
(b) Retired personnel officer placed in a similar post with an industrial training organisation.
(c) Redundant aircraft engineer placed in an accounts post with a furniture manufacturer.
(d) Redundant bank official placed as office manager with a trade federation.
(e) Retired insurance official placed in a clerical post with insurance brokers.
(f) Retired production controller placed in a clerical post with food machinery manufacturers.

The Buretire movement now proudly claims that it specialises in employment for people of pensionable age, who are: willing to work part-time; reliable; not looking for career prospects; experienced; willing to work flexible hours. Buretire deals with clerical, craft, domestic, manual, professional, retail, secretarial and technical staff.

Pensioners' workshops

Apart from the splendid pioneer work done by the Employment Fellowship, other workshops are operated by voluntary organisations all over the country. You can find out if one operates in your area by asking your local office of the CAB, Social Services department, or public library.

A recent TV programme demonstrated such a pensioners' workshop in Milton Keynes, and introduced a man who had no friends or family; he had nothing but weary time on his hands. For him the loneliness was intense, and there were others like him in Milton Keynes. The enthusiastic workshop organiser said that his chief satisfaction lay in seeing how the workshop gave the pensioners an active life after retirement. He said: 'Unless we can keep their minds working, they can quickly lose both interest and capacity. We are open every day, but our workshop is not run on strict factory lines: for example, there is no foreman.' The workers receive nominal wages only, to avoid any reduction in supplementary benefits. Some jobs are repetitive and boring, but the pensioners said they didn't mind that because they were more interested in the companionship. The pensioners' comments included:

'Great place to come for company, and for keeping yourself busy.'
'Especially in the winter time, we have somewhere to go.'
'Money is secondary; we don't have to look at our own four walls all the time.'
'First thing is making friends.'
'Can't just suddenly stop altogether. Must have something to do.'

If it were not for this opportunity of self-help, many of the pensioners would be spending lonely days and evenings in their flats. If there is no workshop in your area, ask the Employment Fellowship if you could help to start one.

Consultancy

Be wary about setting yourself up in your own home as a consultant. You will find that once you have left your employer's office it is very difficult and expensive to keep yourself up to date with trade and professional publications and magazines. It is far better for you if you can obtain employment from other organisations, and can work on a freelance basis. If you set yourself up as a consultant, and *are* successful, this will inevitably bring in its train increased overheads.

Someone like you can help!

If you are interested in voluntary rather than paid employment, go to your local library and consult *The Handbook and Directory of Voluntary Social Services.* This book lists no fewer than 600 voluntary organisations which need help. If there is no local branch of your favourite charity in your area, why not accept the challenge and start one? There is always a need for your help in establishing the missing element.

The Volunteers Advisory Service of the London Council of Social Service (Tel 01-388 0241) can put you in touch with the appropriate local organisation (in London) for advice about voluntary work; but, of course, many of the organisations have a nationwide network (eg Toc H, Dr Barnardo's, Oxfam, People's Dispensary for Sick Animals, Age Concern, etc).

There are over 200 volunteer bureaux throughout the country. Ask your town hall, public library or CAB volunteer if there is a bureau in your area. If there is not, write to the information officer of the chosen volunteer centre HQ stating the district in which you are prepared to offer your services. A stamped, addressed envelope would be appreciated.

Help is needed with advice on housing, baby sitting, catering, clothing collection, gardening, interviewing, languages, marriage guidance, nursing and first aid, playgroups, publicity and public speaking, letter writing and visiting.

In other chapters we have emphasised that we all like to feel that we are necessary to others. During your career, the receipt of your pay slip is a tangible regular reminder that your employer wants you. When you exchange pay packet for pension book, the sense of purpose and of being needed can be eroded.

G Watkin Williams rightly urges: 'Avoid isolation without roots, freedom without responsibility, receiving without giving, leisure without satisfaction, security without self-respect. Do not become a human cabbage — for such a human vegetable is not really a thing of beauty.'

Part-time paid work, voluntary work or, ideally, a combination of both can bridge the gap that can open up when the full-time career ends. Such activities will bring you satisfaction, regular human contacts, dispel loneliness, prevent boredom, and keep you out of the poverty trap.

An essential handbook of voluntary work is the Pan paperback *Working for Free* by Sheila Moore. This is a mine of information, detailing voluntary organisations that give a service or raise funds for others, statutory authorities that recruit volunteers, and self-help or pressure groups.

Voluntary help organisers

Voluntary help organisers assist in most large hospitals. Help is needed at all hours of the day, and night, provided one can offer one's services on a regular basis for more than a couple of hours at a time. Volunteers can operate tea bars, library and shop trolleys. The shop in a hospital is often run by the League of Friends. The Friends' shop, staffed by voluntary helpers, normally gives all proceeds towards patients' amenities. Helpers are needed to first load trolleys in the mornings and to sell in the shop; and later, in the afternoons, to take the trolleys round the wards. Visitors are needed, especially in psychiatric hospitals or wards, for those patients who have no relatives or friends. Tea shops need volunteers not only for people visiting patients and the patients themselves but also for those waiting for x-rays and tests.

Ward receptionists often get a small wage; drivers are required for escorting patients, and the morale of long-term female patients can be improved by beauty care schemes. Enquire at your local hospital or council of voluntary service.

We asked one voluntary help organiser if there was any clash of interests between volunteers and paid staff. She replied, 'We aim to supplement rather than substitute. There is, for example, very little opportunity for a paid member of the staff to spare the time to read or write letters for a patient who has had an eye operation. The voluntary worker can add that extra dimension to a patient's life.'

Watch your local press if you like organising. Today, many voluntary help organisers' posts are salaried.

Rent-a-cook

Opportunities sometimes crop up for housebound women to cash in on their culinary skills.

The demand for home-made pies, cakes and pastries is generally one that, in this mass production age, the bakery trade cannot meet. If you have a skill in this direction, ask your local pastry shop, delicatessen, or hotels if you may supply them. You must be prepared, once you have started, to fulfil your obligations and meet your orders without fail. If you let your customer down just once, you will almost certainly lose the business as he may have already taken orders for your goods.

More ambitious and skilful women have combined to provide a professional cooked gourmet food service. They supply the needs of the hostess who has to give a dinner party in her own home, sometimes at short notice, or help a secretary to provide a business lunch in the office for the boss's guests. By delivering home-made frozen foods that the purchaser can simply heat and serve, they are following the golden rule, 'find a need and create a service'.

Don't undersell yourself. Keep a meticulous account of every penny spent on materials, lighting, cooking, delivery, telephone calls, and postage.

Job Release scheme

The government's Job Release scheme offers a chance for women of 59 and men of 64 years of age to apply for Job Release. The scheme is due to end on 31st March 1979, but we think that with no early solution in sight to the unemployment situation, Job Release is likely to be extended rather than halted.

If your employer agrees to release you, he must also agree to take on someone from the unemployed register. Under the present scheme you will get £26.50 a week *tax free*, and many married people will be eligible for £35. Enquiries should be made at the local office of the Department of Employment, the nearest Jobcentre, or the Unemployment Benefit Office.

This is an opportunity for people who relish the prospect for self-fulfilment which retirement offers. We cannot agree with the comment of the government spokesman who said that it is a nice opportunity to 'put your feet up that much earlier'. Retirement, if viewed in that light, may not last very long.

Franchises

In spite of repeated warnings and legislation designed to protect the unwary, many individuals are continuing to pay large sums for the 'privilege' of participating in franchise schemes. Sadly, one of the effects of present economic conditions, with employees receiving large lump sums when declared redundant, is that they may be tempted to respond to cunningly worded advertisements designed to attract the attention of the man or woman who is psychologically at a low ebb for lack of a job. There is always the attraction of being one's own boss after working for others, and the executive, dispirited when attempts to find alternative employment fail, may see the franchise offer as a white hope offering a good return on an investment. Sometimes the franchise may involve the purchase of stocks of goods and the allocation of exclusive areas in which to operate, backed by 'extensive publicity'.

Some franchise operations are perfectly above board and are, indeed, household names. If you are of retirement age, however, you may find the stress and strain too much. If you can find part-time work in such a business, you will gain an insight into what is involved for the owner.

Consult your bank manager and solicitor before parting with one penny or signing any document.

If you are tempted to work for yourself there is an inexpensive sister publication to this book available from Kogan Page: *Working for Yourself*, by Godfrey Golzen. It includes a chapter devoted to those of retirement age. See Bibliography page 187.

The earnings rule

As we have mentioned earlier, the National Insurance contributory pension is a Retirement Pension, and not an Old Age Pension. Women over 60 and men over 65 receive the pension if they have retired from regular work. Earnings up to a certain level can be disregarded. Up to June 1974, pensioners could only earn a maximum of £9.60 per week without having their Retirement Pension reduced. Fortunately, a continuing campaign by the Pre-Retirement Association and other organisations won the support of individual politicians who believe that the opportunity for pensioners to continue to work part-time is one of the finest ways of avoiding the 'scrap heap' complex. Today, the earnings rule allows a male pensioner and his wife to earn up to £45 per week each without affecting their State Retirement Pension. The rule does not apply to men of 70 or more, or women of 65 or more. Their pensions remain intact whatever their earnings may be.

Occupations in retirement

There may well be retirement opportunities in your area for paid or unpaid work as:

Accountant/book-keeper/VAT adviser

Adult education lecturer

Amateur dramatic society helper — prompting, painting scenery, stage lighting

Appeals organiser for local branches of charities

Auditor

Bursar — school or church

Car, clerical services for hospitals, the handicapped and the aged

Cashier — betting shop

Caterer, social functions

Chairman or member of inquiry tribunals

Church organist — relief work

Coaching for examinations

Consultant, British Executive Service Overseas

Consultant, income tax appeal commission

Counsellor, Marriage Guidance Council

County Charity review officer

Craft teacher

Dressmaker

Editor of information/newsletter/magazines for local church, club or council

Flag day cashier/local organiser

Freelance journalist

Hairdressing (private)

Holiday relief work

Hospital broadcasting service presenter

Industrial relations adviser

Inventory taking

Invigilator

Local government councillor

Market survey work

Meals on Wheels driver or helper

Music teacher

Official of local club/political party, country show

Open University tutor/exam paper marker

Piano tuner

Prison visitor

Proof reader

Receptionist

Recorder for local history or archaeological societies

Red Cross or St John's ambulance worker

Royal Women's Voluntary Service member

School meals supervisor

Secretary/typing work

Shop assistant/cashier

Speaker on cookery, travel,
history, costume, natural
history, to local societies,
Women's Institutes
Steward at concert hall
Stocktaker at weekends
Supervisor, job creation or
special temporary
employment schemes
Supervisor for mechanical, civil,
electrical engineering
apprentices (EIGA scheme)

Training Board committee
member
Translator/interpreter
Treasurer, local club, sports
organisation, Rotary,
Townswomen's Guilds
Tutor, Adult Literacy Campaign
Workers' Education Association
lecturer

Points to remember

1. Part-time paid work can bridge the gap when a full-time career ends — helping finances, providing regular human contacts and preventing boredom.
2. Voluntary work can provide satisfying personal relationships and the opportunity to make a worthwhile contribution to the community.
3. 'Work is hard — no work is harder' (Cypriot saying).

Chapter 8
Living Arrangements

When you first consider the question of retirement housing and get down to essentials, you are faced with an apparently simple choice — you can either stay in the same area or you can move away. The longer you think about it, however, the more you see complications in the basic decision. In our experience, even logically minded, hard-headed businessmen and women fail to apply their usual rational thinking or to exclude sentiment when deciding where they themselves should live in retirement. If, for the best part of 40 years, you have been fighting your way into an office in the centre of London, Glasgow or Leeds, the thought of the release which retirement will bring from stop-start motoring, rail cuts and infrequent buses, is certainly attractive. But if you get the migratory urge, please do pause and consider all the implications before you hastily buy that rose-covered cottage in Devon, or follow some unrealistic wish to return to the place where you were born and spent your childhood. Are you chasing sunbeams in more senses than one? How much will you miss your existing home, on which so much care and money has been lavished to bring it into line with your personal tastes?

Everyone should weigh up their future housing needs some years ahead of retirement. Plans can be worked out in good time and decisions made logically. Once a course of action has been chosen, you have adequate time to implement it. If you choose to stay in the same house, there may be improvements which should be made now, while you are still enjoying a full salary.

If you decide to move, it's the early bird who has the choice of all the titbits on offer from the house agents. It is never too early to explore alternative areas in which to live. There is no point in delaying thought on this matter until you retire and then rushing around expecting to buy your dream house within a few weeks.

As with many decisions concerned with retirement, there is little that is clear-cut. Housing decisions will be affected by many considerations: expense; type of home needed; area, whether city, country or seaside; climate; and friends and family responsibilities. We will put the spotlight in turn on the various alternatives. We hope that this chapter will help you to bring the problem into focus so that, after discussion in detail with your wife, family and friends, you will arrive at the right decision. When you have retired you are going to spend much more time in your own home. If one partner has been persuaded to move, against his or her better judgement, this is almost a guarantee of discord.

Retirement migration

When the authors were with the Pre-Retirement Association they worked with Age Concern to produce a Retirement Migration leaflet (see Bibliography p 187).

If you are married and your children have left home, then possession of a three or four-bedroomed house is an asset which will prove costly in terms of both time and money to maintain and heat it.

One aspect today is that people of retirement age are generally so fit! They move on retirement and may take on a commitment, such as a huge garden, which could force them to make yet another move ten years later when they may not be as energetic, fit and adaptable as they are now.

Gardens

Gardening is one of Britain's most popular leisure activities. Many an office worker looks forward to retirement in order to devote more time to his precious plot, but a garden which gives delight in the 60s can be a burden in your 70s. Digging, stooping, and bending do not get easier with the passage of time. Be prepared for your mobility to decrease gradually with age. A jobbing gardener will be both difficult to find and an expensive luxury on a reduced income. Settle for a home with an easily manageable garden and a greenhouse. Nothing is more depressing for a seventy-year-old house owner than to watch nature taking over a garden on which so much care and money has been lavished. A greenhouse is a fine investment; you will have the time to nurse along those early tomatoes which save the retirement budget many pounds and give so much satisfaction and interest. If you are still keen in your 60s to take on a larger commitment, then do apply in good time for an allotment on which to grow your vegetables. You can easily give up the allotment at a later date. In some areas where people have gardens too large for them, there are garden-sharing schemes in operation. You can ask the Citizens' Advice Bureau, or Friends of the Earth if there is a scheme nearby. Make discreet enquiries if there is anyone living near you who cannot cope with, or no longer has need of, the full use of a large vegetable garden. The Friends of the Earth *Allotments Campaign* Manual has an appendix suggesting that the legal problems which can arise over garden sharing can be avoided by the issue of a licence to occupy.

Bungalow or flat?

Please try and project yourself ahead to the time you will be in your 70s. At present the stairs in your house may present no problems but if you decide to move, consider the merits of a stairless residence. A flat in a modern block with a lift is one alternative, but you run the risk of a noisy neighbour who may wish to use his hi-fi equipment at inconvenient hours. A bungalow, easily maintained without the need to scale ladders, may be the answer.

Stairs can be a hazard in later life. Sixty per cent of domestic accidents are due to women falling — mostly down stairs. Perhaps you are happy in your present house and are reluctant to move to a bungalow or flat. Yet the time may come when a member of the household has difficulty in climbing stairs. There is a possible alternative. You can avoid the trauma associated with a move by installing a domestic staircase lift. Although expensive, it is certainly less than the total cost of moving from a house to a flat or bungalow.

Coast or country

Attracted by the vision of more sunshine on the south coast, you may decide to live on our 'Costa Geriatrica'. If so, you will have to accept the disadvantages of living in an area with an imbalance of population, where the majority are pensioners. Almost certainly, the doctors will be over-worked. Home visits by doctors on the National Health Service are rare because of the strain placed on them by the high proportion of elderly patients on their lists.

The same restrictions will apply to the Social Services, should you need the assistance of a home help in an area swamped by the aged.

If you suffer from asthma or bronchial troubles, do consult your present doctor if you contemplate a move to another area. Obviously your present doctor could also depart, but if you have built up a good relationship with your GP, do seriously consider all the implications of a move away. Not only will you have to alert a new doctor to your problems, but you may face transport problems in getting to his surgery. The same considerations apply if you need specialist advice or treatment from time to time.

The prices in the village shop will be higher than the city supermarket. Despite attempts by small traders to band together, the small shopkeeper cannot hope to match successfully the prices of Sainsbury's and Tesco. You must be prepared to pay more in rustic surroundings.

Write down and assess your present and future priorities. Sample headings should include the following:

Health: Nearness to doctor, hospital, chiropodist, chemist, dentist. Using a car? Without a car?

Accessibility: To shops, post office, library, bank, adult education classes, cinema, restaurant, park, council offices?

Family and friends: Will you still be within reach of them and will they be able to reach you easily? Will your children/friends remain where they are now?

Housing: Stairs? Central heating? (Is gas available?) Double glazing? Roof insulation? Telephone? Expensive maintenance and repairs?

Peace and the countryside are not necessarily synonymous. Once you have pinpointed your area, go and stay in the district for a week or more. A small boarding house is a more likely source of gossip and chat than a hotel, and is perhaps only to be beaten by the pub as a source of information.

Use the opportunity to walk around the districts you like, at all hours of the day. If you are a fanatic who insists on sleeping with windows open at night, check, for example, that the local farmer does not chain up a guard dog at night to deter cattle stealers. You will not enjoy listening to its howling all night. Will you be near an RAF or USAAF base? An artillery range? A field let out to caravanners in the summer? Boarding kennels? A proposed motorway? Buying a pint for a regular in the pub might be a good investment if you ask him a few questions. Most people are flattered if you seek their advice, and some actually relish the opportunity to display their knowledge. Check and double check all items of gossip with, say, the village shop or sub-post office.

Family ties

If you are a member of a fairly close-knit family, do take into account the cost of travelling to see your children and grandchildren. Will they be able to afford the cost of fares to visit you? With the rising cost of travel, this is an important consideration. For pensioners, the British Rail Card for Senior Citizens is a boon, offering half fare anywhere in the UK. If you move, for example, from Birmingham to Barnstaple in retirement you may well find that a pattern emerges in which you spend Christmas at your children's homes, and they make a two weeks' visit to your home during the summer.

The question of family relationships is a serious one. It is your family and friends who rally round in an emergency, and this can be a problem for you and them if you are living hundreds of miles apart. (In chapter 9 we describe the help available from the Social Services and voluntary organisations such as Age Concern, but in cases like the above these services are hard pressed to meet the needs of the elderly.)

Part-time work

We deal with this subject in more detail in chapter 7 so we will touch only briefly on the subject here as far as removal is concerned. Most coastal towns offer part-time work for pensioners only during the holiday season, and even then they have to compete with young students for what little work is available. If you need part-time work to balance the budget, the country and seaside generally have little to offer.

Going up or going down?

We have all met people who seem to be able to buy a property, spend time and trouble on it and a few years later sell the house at a nice tax-free profit. We don't for one moment suggest that this is a suitable retirement occupation. (Continued buying and selling may, anyway, attract the attention of the Inland Revenue if they consider you are making a business of buying and selling.) What is significant is that the people who buy and sell successfully always ensure that the district in which they intend to invest is not going to deteriorate. They try to choose an area in which property will appreciate in value. Before you move away from an area, make sure that the reasons for your move will remain valid. If you are concerned about the construction of a new motorway, check what help the local Council may give you to reduce noise (double glazing, for example). Ask the Council for the free leaflet, *Insulation against Traffic Noise*. Check with the town planning officer at the local Council offices about future plans for the area. Never try to economise in retirement by stopping the local newspaper. It will prove invaluable to you in keeping abreast with local developments. If you really cannot afford the paper, make the local library reading room a regular stop on one of your walks.

So, one of the factors to be considered in deciding whether or not to move is whether your district is changing for the better or worse. Is it going up or going down?

Choosing a new district

Perhaps you bought a house in an urban area many years ago. It has now increased tremendously in value and you are tempted to sell up and move away.

How do you find out prices of properties in different parts of the UK? We suggest you study *Dalton's Weekly* which carries advertisements from all parts of the country. Having pinpointed a suitable area you can then obtain the local paper and make contact with estate agents operating in the area. You will be amazed at the difference in property values of identical houses in different parts of the country.

In March 1978, the National Association of Estate Agents published a guide to current prices. Prices quoted for a pre-war three-bedroomed, semi-detached house with garage and central heating included the following examples:

Bradford, Yorks	£6.625
Edinburgh	£23,250
Derby	£11,250
Plymouth	£14,250
Kingston-on-Thames	£25,500

Suppose you are Mr Footloose of Kingston-on-Thames and are worried, like all of us, about inflation. It is very tempting to decide to move away to, say, Plymouth and pocket a handsome profit.

You have read in an earlier section of the pros and cons of moving away and may still be tempted to uproot yourself. If the financial considerations are tipping the balance, then let us put three points to you — the opportunity for rate rebates from the Council; the opportunity to purchase a mortgage annuity; and the substantial amounts you will have to pay out in the process of buying, selling, moving and settling into the new home.

Rate rebates

You have (we hope) completed the financial exercise suggested in chapter 4. If you have yet to retire, you have a fair idea of what your reduced income will be on retirement. If Mr Footloose chooses to go along to his Council offices to collect a copy of the leaflet *How to Pay Less Rates,* the officials will guide him through the bureaucratic maze of rate rebates. Mr Footloose may then find one financial worry can be reduced. He should not be slow to claim his due. He can then judge how his reduced rates in Kingston compare with a possibly non-reduced rate in Plymouth. (This assumes he has invested his profit on selling his Kingston house. The income from his increased capital may be taken into account in assessing his eligibility for rate relief in his new area.)

Car owners

If you are a car-owner, remember that insurance companies have the right to insist on a medical examination (and at your own expense) at any age from 70 onwards. If you fail, you could be forced to rely on public transport to get you to the shops, the doctor, or the public library. Outside London and other large cities, reduced bus fares are a rarity and our guess is that Britain will follow the American pattern of a diminishing bus service. So please make sure that your new home has the essential shops nearby and that you are not completely dependent on private transport. Couples should make sure that, wherever possible, both partners can drive a car.

Buying and selling expenses

It is estimated that the average cost of buying and selling a property valued at £20,000 will be in the region of £1,500. Estate agents, solicitors, surveyors, stamp duty, removals, and insurance, will all stake a claim and their combined costs will be a significant factor in estimating any surplus you might hope to achieve in moving from one district to another.

Shop around for estate agents. There is no longer any conformity in their scales of charges. Read very carefully any agreement you may be asked to sign. If you wish you can put the property in the hands of a number of agents, but make this clear to each of them at the time. You may decide to try selling your house yourself. Sometimes it may seem that the agents do reap a disproportionately high figure for the work involved. Often, however, agents have many disappointments and incur expenses in advertising before they succeed in finding a willing purchaser who then successfully negotiates a mortgage. For a house owner on the point of retirement, we consider, on balance, the services of an estate agent justified. Putting your house on offer and consequently having to show strangers over your home can be a disturbing and time-consuming experience. Use the experts, but we suggest the agents you choose should be members of the appropriate professional association, The Royal Institution of Chartered Surveyors or The Incorporated Society of Valuers and Auctioneers.

We asked a London firm of estate agents what advice they could give to purchasers of property. They always tell prospective purchasers to get out of their cars, and walk around the district. This makes particularly good sense to those approaching retirement. You not only see things you would miss by driving through the area but you get the feel of the area and notice the hills! This is an essential point when you are projecting yourself to the time when you will be 70-plus years of age. The day may come, for various reasons, when you have to walk everywhere. In retirement, it would be nice to be within easy walking distance of the shops and a post office, and to be able to use public transport to the doctor, the dentist and the library. The rose-covered cottage on top of the hill may seem idyllic now, but it can become a prison if you are no longer able to drive.

Solicitors' charges may also vary on house sale and purchase. If you have friends who used solicitors and estate agents in the area, ask them whether they were dealt with expeditiously and economically.

When buying a new property you have some protection, if the house is covered by the National House-Building Council scheme. The cover under the 10-year guarantee against major defects is limited, however, to the amount which repairs would have cost at the date the certificate for the house was issued. You will be well advised to cover the costs of inflation by insurance, and indeed some building societies insist on this before granting a mortgage. Building society managers will give their advice free of charge on such matters. For example, the Abbey National Building Society issues a free booklet on home ownership.

It is also important to visit an area at different times of the year or even different weeks. Stay there for a week or so (out of season if it is a holiday resort) and make yourself familiar with the area and the facilities available. The coastal town, bright with flowers and shops with coloured awnings, can be a very different place in the winter with biting winds, high seas washing over the promenade and 90 per cent of shops and hotels shut. Similarly, the quiet turning off the high street visited on a week day in the spring can become jammed as a parking lot for shoppers on a Saturday, or all week in the summer for holiday makers.

Surveys

Always have a property structurally surveyed before buying. Even a modern flat can incur high maintenance costs.

Incidentally, top-floor flats with flat roofs can be particularly troublesome, being prone to letting in rain. Top-floor flats also often suffer from poor thermal insulation and this can lead to condensation problems. Flats on the second floor or above, which lack lifts, are really unsuitable for the elderly or for parents with young children. If you employ a surveyor, a local man can be invaluable because of his close knowledge of both the properties and the area.

Most surveyors will tell you that a top floor has but one advantage. There is no noise from the flat above!

When discussing estate agents we suggested it might be prudent to check that they are members of the Royal Institution of Chartered Surveyors or Incorporated Society of Valuers and Auctioneers. For survey work this is essential.

A business with accommodation

Many people long to leave paid employment and to enter into business on their own account. Another book by Godfrey Golzen, *Working for Yourself*, published by Kogan Page deals with this subject in detail. One of the authors contributed the Retirement chapter. From the housing angle a shop with living accommodation above poses many problems for a couple in their 60s. Ill-health or death of one of the partners can result in the hasty sale of a business and the need to find other accommodation. Not a good recipe, we fear, for a happy retirement!

Caravans or mobile homes

We know that caravanning is a very popular pastime and many pensioners own caravans sited at the seaside or in the country for summer use. We do not recommend a caravan for round-the-year living for those aged 60 upwards. If you are a confirmed addict, however, we suggest you subscribe to the monthly *Mobile Home*. If you want to use a mobile home as a permanent residence on your own land, you will first require planning permission and a site licence from the local council. If you want to keep it on an established site, make sure that the site owner has all necessary permissions and find out what conditions he attaches to the letting agreement. It is essential that you go through all the necessary preliminaries to secure your site before you invest in a mobile home.

Staying put

Perhaps you have brought up a family in one of those large Victorian three-storey houses. Your children have grown up and left home. The house is now much too big for one or two persons. You have considered all the obvious alternatives, including selling the house, and have decided to stay where you are. Let us run through some of the things you might like to consider to bring in some much needed cash, or allow you to improve the property.

LETTING ROOMS

You may be married, and needing some extra income. You may be single or widowed, and may still need extra cash, and perhaps enjoy some company at the same time. It must be remembered that the net income received from any sub-tenants is taxable. The income may also come within the provisions of the earnings rule if you are between 60 and 65 (female) and 65 and 70 (male). You may be worried about taking in lodgers; you have heard of cases of landlords sub-letting and not being able to evict unsuitable tenants because of the workings of the Rent Acts. Do not dismiss the idea outright. There are still realistic possibilities open to you if you are prepared to open your house to strangers. Technically, tenants of all accommodation have only limited rights of security if the landlord or landlady is resident, so the provision of a service, such as breakfast, is not essential.

You may have a university or a polytechnic near you which needs rooms for limited periods for students. We know of one unmarried business woman living in London who has made an arrangement with a language school to accommodate students. The school is constantly receiving students from all over the world who come to London for, on average, a study period of four weeks. The only obligation on the part of the landlady is to provide bed and breakfast. The landlady, who has a full-time job, receives £25 per week for each student (usually adults). If she wishes, she can make her own financial arrangements for providing extra meals for her guests. This scheme has worked very well for her — providing income, an interest, and company. One student from Germany has returned for a refresher course and the landlady has been invited to spend a holiday in the home of the student's parents in the Black Forest. Now that she is nearing retirement age, she is seriously looking around to buy a larger house so that she may take more students, and increase her income.

Do proceed with caution regarding any type of letting arrangement, however, because there can be some discrepancy between theory and practice in evicting tenants. Remember the local Citizens' Advice Bureau can always help you if you have any difficulties. They can supply the official leaflets *Rooms to Let, Landlords and the Law, Letting your own Home* and *Shared Houses*. Raise queries with the CAB, however, *before* you take in guests.

If you live in the London area and think that a civil servant would be an appropriate paying guest, then you could contact the bureau specially set up to deal with the problem of housing civil servants who are brought to London from the provinces. You may be able to let rooms to a civil servant who will normally return to his own home each week-end. However, do remember that if you sell the property at some future date, you may be liable to pay Capital Gains Tax on those parts of the house you have let.

Your local Rent Office can give you an idea of the demand for accommodation in your area and an indication of an acceptable rent. Further information can be obtained from the Houseowners' Association.

You may decide that another way to reduce costs is to invite your sister, cousin or a close friend to come and live in the house and to share the overheads. Beware of sharing kitchen facilities. The Poles have an expression: 'Guests are like fish — after three days they stink'. This may either amuse or shock you, but there is usually a grain of truth in such sayings. If you are planning an arrangement like this, make sure all details are settled and agreed beforehand.

LETTINGS – HOLIDAYS
If you live in a holiday area, then a series of short lets throughout the summer can be quite lucrative. You may consider going abroad for a year to stay with a son or daughter who has emigrated. If you are worried about the effects of a long let, then ask your local estate agents if there is a demand for furnished accommodation by companies or foreign embassies. In many areas there is a constant demand for units of accommodation to be rented for one to two years. Lettings

on this basis are ideal. You can take a breathing space between lets and reassess the rent each time in the light of inflation.

HOUSE IMPROVEMENTS AND CONVERSIONS
If you live in an older home, which lacks certain amenities, you may be considering a move to a more modern one. But the local Council may be ready to give you (not lend you) money in the shape of a grant, towards the cost of work which may be needed to raise the standard of your existing home or to keep it in good repair. This alternative may be less expensive for you than the cost of moving.

Advice on what is available in grants can be obtained from the local Council offices or town hall. The Department of the Environment has issued local government offices and Citizens' Advice Bureaux with copies of the free leaflet *Your Guide to House Renovation Grants*. Ask for a copy if you are interested in the idea.

You are not asking for charity if you apply for a grant — the government was so concerned at the lack of response by house owners in applying for grants that in March 1978 it spent £300,000 on a campaign to publicise the various schemes available. It is far cheaper for the government to encourage private house owners to improve their properties than to have homes decay so that ultimately they have to be replaced by Council houses.

It may come as a shock to learn that, in 1978, 800,000 homes in England alone were considered unfit to live in, and an additional 900,000 houses lacked such ordinary amenities as a bathroom, indoor lavatory and hot and cold water.

There are four different types of grant, but the more common are known as 'intermediate grants' and 'improvement grants'. Intermediate grants are made to help meet the cost of improving houses by providing certain missing standard amenities (for example, a bathroom, an inside WC, a hot and cold water supply, etc) coupled with essential repairs and replacements. (There are a number of requirements which have to be met in order to qualify for an intermediate grant, but if the conditions are satisfied, the Council cannot refuse a valid application.) Improvement grants are made at the discretion of the local Council, to help owners improve older houses to a good standard, or for converting properties into flats.

125

For each type of grant there is an upper limit of costs which may be grant-aided (called the 'eligible expense'). The grant made is a percentage of the 'eligible expense' and in most cases is 50 per cent, although in some circumstances it could be higher. One couple we know in a certain area in the north of England took over a 'Coronation Street' type of residence and later collected a 75 per cent grant towards the cost of installing an indoor toilet, bathroom and hot and cold water supply.

If, as the owner of the property, you are short of the balance of money needed to complete the work, a loan may also be forthcoming from the local Council to cover your share of the costs. You can also try your bank or building society. After all, you are seeking to improve the property and increase its capital value.

If you own such a property, and decide to convert or improve it, do not authorise a builder to proceed with the work until you are satisfied that you have the formal consent of the local Council as regards the grant, planning approval, and approval under the building regulations. The Council will also want you to get detailed quotations for the work, for their approval, before you make any commitments. Surveyors' fees attract grant aid up to the grant limit.

Every local authority has an Environmental Health Officer. His advice on grants and what is needed to improve or repair the structure of your home is free, whether you are a home owner or a tenant.

The bad news is that the improvement of a house may well increase the total rates payable.

Before receiving a grant, you have to provide a certificate of future occupation. Conditions are attached to the grant which are intended to ensure that for a period, normally five years, the home is used in the manner described in your certificate. In some cases the Council may demand repayment of all or a part of the grant if there is a breach of the conditions. (For example, if you use it as a second home.) So if it is your intention to sell your property shortly after a conversion, check carefully with the Council.

Give your house away and live rent free!

You may have reached a stage in life when you find yourself

living alone in a large house. You may not have any surviving relatives or close friends, and your problems are aggravated by the worries that house ownership entails — expensive upkeep and repairs. You may have no one to whom to bequeath the house after your death. Your problems might be solved by offering the house as a gift to Help the Aged. This movement claims to be the largest fund-raising organisation working for old people. If Help the Aged take over your house they will, in return, convert part of it into a flat in which you can live rent and rate-free for life. The scheme allows the donor to be freed from financial problems without having to move away. Once a person has agreed to donate a property, Help the Aged will undertake to employ professional architects to plan the conversion, be responsible for insurance and external maintenance, pay legal fees and advise donors on Capital Gains Tax. Details are available from the Honorary Director of Housing, Help the Aged.

Try to visualise your home after conversion. You will have other people living in closer proximity than before. Ask Help the Aged for examples of completed conversions, and talk to people who have participated in the scheme.

MORTGAGE ANNUITIES

Many people expect to have paid off the mortgage on their house by the time they reach retirement age. Their home probably represents their most valuable capital asset.

Perhaps our friend, Mr Footloose, bought his Kingston house many years ago for £10,000. His mortgage is paid off and he sees the prospect of collecting £25,000 (less fees and expenses) as tempting. He and his wife, being a sensible couple, have discussed whether they wish to bequeath their house to their only son, Nigel. They have decided there is no real need to worry about this. Nigel, benefiting from a good education, is already an Executive Officer in the Civil Service, and has a guaranteed inflation-proof pension to look forward to. Nigel's wife intends to return to full-time teaching when their only child reaches school age. Any cash left to Nigel after the death of his parents will therefore be regarded as a bonus and not a necessity. The son of the family would be the last person to expect his parents to make any sacrifices during their retirement.

Mr Footloose (like others) is advised to look into the

possibility of taking out a mortgage annuity on his present home.

Two companies, the Save & Prosper Group and Hambro Provident Assurance Ltd, are prepared to advance sums of money to older persons against the security of their home. In Mr Footloose's case he could well be advanced £10,000 against the value of his £25,000 property. (Generally speaking an insurance company will advance up to 75 per cent of the current value.) This sum is automatically placed by the company towards an annuity. The company calculates the interest due on the loan and sends a cheque each month for the annuity less the loan interest. The annuity is payable to Mr Footloose and, on his death, to his widow (or vice versa). Because of the tax situation, the annuity provides Mr Footloose and his wife with much needed income for the rest of their lives. (He can claim tax relief on the mortgage interest.) On the death of the surviving partner, the house is sold, the mortgage paid off and the balance distributed to the beneficiaries of the estate. In this way, the ever-increasing value of the house, due to inflation, is passed on to the estate.

For further information about these schemes send a stamped addressed envelope to The Life Offices' Association, quote *Focus on Retirement* and ask for the list of member companies offering mortgage annuities. When you receive the details we suggest you then write to the companies operating the scheme and ask for an estimate. The extra income will vary according to whether you are married or single, your present age, the value of your property, and the rate of tax. As an example, however, a single man of 65 could collect something in the region of an extra £7 per week for life. It's worth thinking about it, and possibly less trouble is involved than in sharing your home!

We do *not* recommend alternative plans which involve the transfer of the house to a company. This allows the original owners to continue to live in the house for the remainder of their lives, but deprives them of the right to benefit from any increase in the value of the property and destroys flexibility, as the original owner cannot move away from the house if personal circumstances change.

So, please do not disregard rate rebates or mortgage annuities if finance is one of the reasons prompting you to sell up and move away from home.

BECOME A COUNCIL TENANT?

In some areas Councils operate an enlightened scheme which is attractive to house owners of retirement age. Councils are sometimes prepared to buy a large privately-owned house at a figure to be assessed by independent valuation. Under the arrangement, the house owner is granted the tenancy of a smaller rented Council flat. This gives the former owner the chance to continue living in the same district, gain a secure tenancy, and realise his capital. Not all Councils are so helpful, but it costs nothing to enquire at the town hall. There may also be a local housing association in your area, operating a similar scheme.

EXISTING COUNCIL TENANTS

About 50 per cent of the population live in rented accommodation of one kind or another. If you live in Council accommodation, then you do not have such freedom of action in changing your house on retirement, but alternatives are still open to you. If you rent a large house, the Council will usually be pleased to take your home back into their housing pool so that they can offer it to a young couple with a growing family. In exchange, they may offer you a more suitable place, such as a ground-floor flat, or purpose-built accommodation for older people.

If you live in a large city and would like to move to, say, Worthing, then you can advertise in the Worthing press and in local shop windows, in the hope of securing an exchange. Ask at your Council housing office if they know of any person wishing to move to your area. Papers such as *Dalton's Weekly* also carry advertisements from people seeking exchanges.

Some of the larger authorities, including London, control property in seaside or country areas such as Hastings and Milton Keynes, and may be able to re-house you. If you live in Greater London, write to County Hall for details of the 'Seaside and Country Accommodation scheme'. Enquire in good time as there is a long waiting-list. If the move is not successful, or circumstances change, for example with the death of one partner, the Council will also try to re-house you again, back in the London area.

If you are a Council tenant and your income drops on retirement, ask the Citizens' Advice Bureau for the leaflet

There's Money off Rent. You may be entitled to a rent rebate to reduce the amount of rent payable. Entitlement to a rent rebate depends upon a tenant's average earnings, the size of the family (ie number of dependants), and the amount of rent paid (after deducting anything which may be included for rates, furniture, heating, services, etc). The local rent rebates officer is there to help and advise.

TENANTS (NON-COUNCIL HOUSE)

You may rent accommodation from a private landlord or a housing association. If so, and your income is below a certain level, you are similarly entitled to claim a rate rebate and also to apply for a rent allowance. Here again, you can enquire at your local Council offices or town hall. Entitlement to a rent allowance depends on much the same rules as those for rent rebates. The main difference between the two is that the Council is able to deduct a rent rebate direct from a Council tenant's rent but has to pay the allowance to the tenant where there is a private landlord.

If you are a private tenant, there may be some unexpected development which could land you in a situation where you have to find other accommodation (ie you may rent only part of a house and the ownership might change). But remember, you are entitled to proper notice, and it is well worthwhile obtaining expert advice regarding your rights before vacating the property. Incidentally, it costs nothing to register your name on the local Council housing list. Do it *now* and this might prove to be a blessing for you in the years to come.

Safety in the home

Although we all know that road accidents are alarming and frequent, it is nevertheless a fact that most accidents happen in the home.

Once you have decided what type of house you wish to spend your retirement years in, lose no time in making it as safe as possible.

More than one in three accidental fires in the home are due to cookers. The main cause is burning fat. You may, while cooking, be called to the front door and return to the kitchen to find it ablaze. Take the pan off the ring when you leave the kitchen. Tudor Safety Products make a special glass fabric cloth to smother a fire. (Enquire at your ironmonger; price about £5.20p.) If you consider this expensive, keep a large damp cloth or large pan lid handy to smother any burning pan. *Do not use water on a fire caused by fat.*

Do get your electric wiring system checked and, if you live in an older house, have it converted to the 13 amp ring main system. Avoid the temptation to run three flexes off the same electric plug, or to hide wires under carpets. When the TV is switched off, get into the habit of pulling the plug away from the wall socket.

Make sure your electric blankets are returned regularly during the summer months to the makers for overhaul and checking. There is danger for pensioners in using oil stoves but if you must use one, *do* keep the paraffin in a metal container *outside* the house.

A tumble of any kind can destroy confidence in balance and agility. Never try to economise by using low wattage lamps on landings, passages or staircases, and ruthlessly throw away those treasured comfortable slippers which slip through wear. Fasten down any loose stair carpets or other floor coverings which might trip you in an unwary moment. Standing on rickety chairs to reach things stored in high cupboards is another risk to be avoided.

With advancing age, eyesight and hearing begin to deteriorate somewhat, and reactions may become more sluggish. This may lead to more accidents, but much can be done to ensure safety by making the home both snug and safe.

Make it a routine to keep all poisons and medicines in clearly labelled containers, and away from inquisitive grandchildren who may arrive for a visit at short notice.

If you have no knowledge of first aid, why not attend a course in the subject? You will then have more confidence in coping with an emergency. Enquire of your local adult education college or the St John Ambulance Brigade (London headquarters Tel 01-580 6762).

House owners insurance

One of the authors, giving a talk at a pre-retirement seminar, touched on the subject of house insurance and the need to keep the sum insured at a realistic level, both in respect of the house itself and its contents.

It is always helpful in a seminar if any point in a talk is reinforced spontaneously by a member of the audience. In this instance, an unmarried lady civil servant had a sad tale to relate. She was living in London with two years to go to retirement. She had bought an old cottage on the south coast, and had planned to move there after modernisation work was completed. She intended to travel up to town for the two years so that by the time retirement arrived, she would have found friends and interests in the coastal town of her choice. All sound thinking, but a good theory was ruined by a sad stroke of fate. During the evening of the very day on which the workmen completed the renovation of the cottage, fire gutted the entire premises. Insurance? Yes, but she had only insured the cottage for the sum she had paid for the property. The thousands of pounds she spent on modernisation and fittings were not covered by insurance and this deficit represented a complete loss. Her retirement dreams were shattered.

The moral of this tale is to remind you to reconsider annually the amount for which your house is covered by insurance. The insurance companies continually give us this advice, but most of us, made cynical by advertising or from sheer inertia, tend to reject it.

The British Insurance Association is producing leaflets to provide guidance to house owners on the level of inflation affecting costs of rebuilding houses.

Let us turn our thoughts to your insurance cover on the contents. According to a recent *Financial Times* article, the average *replacement* cost of the *contents* of an ordinary three-bedroomed suburban home is £8,500. This, at first sight, may be a rather shattering figure when you tot up the prices you paid for your furniture over the years. May we suggest you take a walk around a local furniture store, and then assess the replacement costs of your possessions. The key word is, of course, *replacement* value. Most policies only cover the written down value of your possessions. If, for example, you have paid, over the years, £4,000 for your household contents, the insurance company could well depreciate the assets to £2,500. Yet, on today's prices, the cost of replacing on a 'new for old' basis could be the average we quoted, ie £8,500.

The cost of such insurance is inevitably higher but the insurance companies are becoming increasingly tough with claimants who have refused to bring their premiums and the sum insured up to current values. The replacement-type insurance will cost you much more than the conventional type of policy, but if you want peace of mind you can ask a local insurance broker to obtain quotations.

HOLIDAY INSURANCE

To prove that we personally have learned the facts of life the hard way, may we tell you that one of the authors had his camera stolen on the first day of his holiday in Romania. The camera was an expensive model, bought duty free when the owner was resident overseas. Then came the time (too late, alas!) to read the small print on the policy issued by the package holiday operators' own insurance company. There was a limit to be claimed on any one item. The upper limit payable by the company on the camera and its accessories was £75 whereas replacement cost was £250. So, if you intend to travel with something valuable like expensive cameras or jewellery, it is best to make sure it is covered in the 'All Risks' section of your normal comprehensive policy.

Equally, if you intend to take advantage of the special-priced holidays offered to pensioners, do be sure to read the insurance policy rules regarding health, especially if you have any history of illness. You may find that you are required to sign a declaration of good health which could debar you from making a claim subsequently. Your own insurance company may treat you more favourably. If you are a BUPA subscriber, take a look at their special policy to cover health risks when travelling overseas.

Security

In 1977, over a quarter of a million thefts from private houses were reported in England and Wales. Most occur during the daytime, and a thief can be in and out of the house in less than three minutes. Usually, the occupant has neglected to secure windows, or back or side doors.

Lock up your home securely when you go out. In the evenings, leave a light on in the lounge (not the hall). Check that your locks conform to British Standards BSS 3621/23.

If you move to another house, it is a wise precaution to instal new exterior locks. Always check the identify of callers, and report anything suspicious to the police. A police car can be at your house within a few minutes. The police can also arrange for a Crime Prevention Officer to give you his professional advice and recommendations on security of your home, if you are worried about it.

Insurance cannot fully compensate for the loss of personal valuables and peace of mind, so take care!

Living abroad (or the last resort!)

As soon as Christmas is over the alluring advertisements for holidays abroad begin. Many have responded in the past to such inducements and enjoyed holidays overseas. Some in the older age bracket may be attracted to the smaller advertisements which continue throughout the year and are designed to induce people to buy a retirement home overseas. The attractions of a modern bungalow in the sun are obvious. Garnish the dish with promises of reduced fuel costs, lower cost of living, little or no taxes and cheap booze and before you know where you are you have yielded to the temptation and clipped out the coupon offering you a free inspection flight. (Free, that is, if you buy a property!)

Many British people have retired happily overseas. Others are caught in a poverty trap. (Until agreement was reached between Spain and the UK, for instance, hundreds of expatriates were drawing UK State Retirement Pensions pegged at the level payable when they emigrated.) If the UK State Retirement Pension is an essential part of your income, it is important to choose a country where you will benefit from increases in the rate.

We spoke to a vigorous 70-year-old who retired to Portugal 10 years ago. Although he still enjoyed the Algarve in many ways, he was beginning to have health problems. The local Portuguese doctor was prescribing pills which were expensive and not fully effective. The pensioner had been urged by a retired British medical practitioner living nearby to return to the UK to live, in order to benefit from the National Health Service and Social Services. (The DHSS issue a leaflet NI38 dealing with health services here.) The pensioner was doubtful, however, about his ability to sell his property for a price sufficient to set up a home again in the UK. He found the Portuguese a friendly people, but discovered that most 'Brits' learnt only a smattering of the language, enough to enable them to buy fruit and vegetables at the market. Unless emigrants are prepared to be at a disadvantage, they should study the language of the country of their adoption so that they are fluent. Without this, they are limited to a small social circle of other expatriates, listening to the BBC World Service, reading the overseas *Daily Telegraph*, and reminiscing about the past. Most of us would find prolonged exposure to such a daily round very boring.

One couple we know bought a flat in Famagusta in Cyprus in 1970. At first, this was a good investment. The flat was managed by agents and let to holiday makers for most of the season. It was also available to the owners for the use of their own family. Then in 1974 the island became a battleground. Famagusta is now in the Turkish Zone and there is no promise of compensation. The lucrative investment of thousands of pounds has become a millstone round their necks. The disillusioned owners told us, 'A major factor influencing the decision to invest in Cyprus at the time was that the island was in the sterling bloc, and the British government were Trustees, an apparent factor of stability. In the event, the British government has taken a very low profile and has consistently absolved itself of any liability'.

If you are sufficiently well-heeled financially both to retain a home in the UK and purchase a villa or flat overseas, and if you proceed with caution, you may be able to enjoy the best of both worlds.

If you are determined to consider retirement overseas, consult your local bank manager in the first instance. Given previous warning of your intentions, he will tell you about the dollar or currency premium payable to purchase the prospective property abroad. He will also advise you of the latest regulations concerning the transfer of sterling overseas by persons emigrating. If you become non-resident for UK tax purposes, then the periods you stay in the UK on return visits will be limited. Your bank manager will be able to supply you with the Bank of England booklet *A Guide to Emigrants.*

Ask your local office of the Department of Health and Social Security office for leaflet SA29. This will tell you the procedure for payment of your state pension abroad and, more important, whether or not you will be eligible to participate in future increases. Such increases are restricted to countries having reciprocal agreements with the UK. If the local office does not have the leaflet, they will obtain it for you from the Department of Health and Social Security headquarters in Newcastle. If you have further questions the Newcastle headquarters has an Overseas Department. Always quote your National Insurance number in correspondence.

We suggest that on release from a long working life you take a well-earned rest. A world cruise or a prolonged tour overseas may enable you to make final decisions about your future. There should be no sudden decision to move away from friends, children and grandchildren. The business man exasperated with form filling will find to his chagrin that permanent emigration overseas will result in yet more paperwork.

Points to remember

1. Assess dispassionately and realistically your housing requirements. Ensure your retirement home is economic to heat, offers privacy, is safe, and well lit. Invest in labour-saving devices.
2. Decide upon the area. Consider:
     Family and friends.
     Medical and support services.
     Climate.
     Local terrain and public transport.
     Accessibility to shops, services and recreational facilities.
     Size of garden.
3. Emigrating?
     Take professional advice.
     Consider language and psychological difficulties, climate, medical facilities, finance, and isolation from family and friends.

Chapter 9

Retirement Housing

Retirement homes

Some years ago one of the authors took a look at retirement homes in the USA. He went there expecting to find retirement ghettoes populated by dreary geriatrics. He was ready to criticise, ready to find fault and only too ready to say, 'I told you so'. Events proved his pre-conceptions to be mistaken. He came away prepared to believe that a modified form of retirement housing could be adopted successfully in the UK, and he is pleased to see that such transplants are now, after painstaking research, coming to fruition over here.

In the United States he found that often the worst type of retirement homes were those run purely for profit, and the best were those run by non-profit-making organisations. Some commercial operators played on the fear of elderly people living in densely populated urban areas, where muggings and thefts were all too common.

Elderly Americans are lured by advertisements for retirement centres offering 'tender loving care', security and sunshine in pollution-free areas of such states as Florida, Arizona and California. Some retirement villages stand in acres of grounds complete with golf courses, tennis and shuffle board courts. Others are in cities such as San Francisco, and comprise high-rise blocks of flats with security guards at the entrance screening all visitors.

It will suffice to describe one such home that had the most desirable features. This is a village nestling in the foothills of Northern California, and run by a religious organisation on a non-profit basis. The village is open to all races and creeds, and naturally has a long waiting list. The author had an introduction to a lady, English by birth, who had lived there for some years. He had a long talk with the lady resident, and an interview with the administrator of the community. The lady occupied a studio apartment with a private patio and a kitchenette. She took most meals in the dining room, where all meals were served by young students from a nearby college. Rooms were available for the entertainment of guests. She was delighted with her decision to enter the Centre. Later on the administrator explained that the philosophy of the community was to make the residents as independent as possible. In the USA the retirement communities had been preceded by charitable homes, and though the new communities were self-supporting some new arrivals tended to think of them as old folks' homes. The administrator discouraged any tendency for the residents to assume a paternalism on the part of the Centre. The residents had therefore formed their own association to develop a policy of self-help. For example, the administrator had ordered the re-surfacing of a disused shuffle board area. No sooner had the work been completed than one of the residents came into his office and said, 'I have been appointed chairman of the Residents' Shuffle Board Committee and I want to tell you how we are going to organise it'. The administrator was delighted to hand over the responsibility.

It was clear that this place offered its residents the opportunity to participate in a full and active life, and allowed them to assume responsibilities towards their fellow residents.

The author concerned was excited when some years ago he was approached, in the offices of the Pre-Retirement Association, by Maitland Cook, Director of the Retirement Homes Association. He, too, had travelled to the US and inside Europe, and after three years of study and research was preparing to launch a new concept for housing and care of people in retirement in the UK. Mr Cook had long been involved professionally with nursing homes, and was appalled by the number of *active* people forced to live in such homes because no realistic alternative existed. Many house-owners on retirement weigh up their house-ownership in the light of continuing inflation, their home having tied up all their capital, being too large for comfort, and continually consuming ever-increasing sums for lighting and heating. Unfortunately, there are sometimes health problems as people grow older. With reduced mobility, this can lead to depression, loneliness and a feeling of helplessness. We all know of aged relatives and friends who lack care and attention, with sad consequences for everyone involved. The Department of Health and Social Security has long acknowledged the existence of the problem, and in its publication *Priorities for Health and Personal Social Services in England* it states: 'The general aim and policy is to help the elderly to maintain independent lives in their own homes for as long as possible.'

As long ago as 1962 it was stated that sheltered accommodation should largely replace one-owner residential homes, and later the idea of 'supported independency dwellings' was introduced. Mr Cook's famous namesake pioneered sea-going routes many years ago. Maitland Cook decided to pioneer (at Southdowns, South Darenth, in Kent) his plan for people over 60 to enjoy 'supported independence within the privacy of the home'.

The Retirement Homes Association provides housing in the form of apartments, bungalows, or in some instances, houses, in which people can live quite privately and independently. These custom-built units are sited together to form a community of people, living together but totally independent of each other. This development is supported by facilities and amenities which can be used or not, as the individual wishes. The estate is run by an administration team which is operational 24 hours per day, seven days a week, to ensure that help is available for any domestic problems that may arise. There is a medical service with a nurse on duty at all times, supported by doctors whose group practice holds a surgery in the estate.

These two services are activated by an emergency alarm system installed in each apartment, so that residents can contact the emergency services at any time, and are safe in the knowledge of total security.

There is a social club and restaurant. This restaurant provides meals as required by the residents, including continental breakfasts, but its main function is to serve as a centre for all leisure and social activities. Its facilities include a licensed bar, dancing, bridge, chess and other activities the residents may wish to pursue. These amenities can also be used by the local people and organisations to ensure that the residents on the estate have the opportunity to become integrated into the local community.

There is also a variety of facilities at Southdowns providing hobby centres, including woodworking and engineering workshops. A lecture room is available so that painting, sewing and flower arranging classes can be organised. Mr Cook has further sites in view, and at every site a hobbies centre will be incorporated to ensure that the residents can pursue their own interests and leisure activities.

Other services include building maintenance, gardening, domestic cleaning, laundry, rubbish collection, and a shopping and provisions service.

The gymnasium can be used for badminton, tennis, and general physical exercise. It is regularly used by the local sports clubs, so that the residents can watch organised sporting activities. We were pleased to see that, as with the American retirement village, residents had the opportunity to become involved with young people.

The outdoor sporting facilities are also used by local sportsmen and include cricket and football fields. Croquet lawns and bowling greens will soon be added.

The church, built in Victorian times, is interdenominational and is available to all residents.

There are allotments for all those who wish to grow their own flowers and vegetable produce. Again, on the American pattern, Mr Cook is most anxious that as residents move in, they should take over the running of as many of the leisure activities as possible. It is alien to the thinking of the Retirement Homes Association that they should lay down specific activities that must be carried out. It is for the residents to decide their own interests and to pursue them, using the facilities provided.

Southdowns is located within 40 minutes of London by train, yet is in the heart of the country. It is ideal in size, as plans exist to develop approximately 150 apartments, an optimum number for this type of scheme. It is well established as a beautifully landscaped estate and the apartments are sited so as to take maximum advantage of the splended Kent countryside. There are private estate roads and pathways, a number of lock-up garages and adequate car parking.

Accommodation units are self-contained and include large living rooms, fully fitted modern kitchens, one or two bedrooms and well equipped bathrooms. Every room has radiator central heating and all apartments have waist level power points, personal alarm systems, baths with grab rails, easy to clean surfaces and unrestricted access. The units are not furnished, because the apartment becomes a person's home and, therefore, must be furnished according to personal tastes and wishes.

All these facilities are provided for the residents, yet they have all options open to them. They can live privately and independently and they can enjoy the leisure and group facilities. They can also use all the service amenities.

The writer asked Mr Cook: 'What is the catch? What do the residents have to pay? What are their liabilities?' He explained that the apartments are licensed to an individual, or couple, for life. The licence is purchased and the capital sum reverts in full on departure or death.

The administration of services is carried out by The Retirement Homes Association on an 'at cost' basis and levied by quarterly management charges. Estimated charges are published in advance and audited accounts are available for inspection, so that the residents can carry out a check.

We then got down to running costs: this is, of course, the crucial question. Mr Cook believes that the cost of living on an RHA estate is attractive. The licence fees range between £9,000 and £13,000 depending on the size of the unit. As property prices in most areas are considerably higher than this, the individual or couple selling their house and moving to a Retirement Homes Association scheme, will be releasing a substantial part of their capital to assist in the enjoyment of their retirement years.

It is estimated that the management charge will range between £630 and £1,130 per annum (1978 figures) depending on the size of the apartment occupied. This charge includes rates, water rates, total maintenance, gardening, medical and warden services, central heating, domestic cleaning, rubbish disposal, laundry and all the other facilities provided on the estate. The only direct costs incurred by the residents are for lighting, hot water and cooking, which allows a substantial saving on the provision of these facilities in conventional surroundings.

This whole scheme, from its inception to fruition, is the work of private investment. Mr Cook, not surprisingly, is a firm believer in private enterprise, but he has thanked the Department of Health and Social Security, the Pre-Retirement Association, and Kent County Council's Social Services Department for their help and interest in formulating the scheme.

The first batch of homes at Southdowns were sold out before the opening day, and the Retirement Homes Association is now actively developing other sites.

We have described the Southdowns scheme in some detail as it seems to us to be one of the most far-sighted and ambitious developments so far undertaken in the UK. However, there are many other forms of housing designed or adapted for use by retired people. You can find out what may be available in your own area by asking at your local Council offices. We have included a list of addresses, including the Retirement Homes Association, at the end of this book.

Sheltered housing

Immediately following the war years, local authorities concentrated on building houses for couples with young families. Most Council housing estates built at that time consisted predominantly of two or three-bedroomed houses. By the 1950s, local authorities began to realise that there was also a need for a different type of accommodation suited to the needs of older people. In many cases, the light dawned only when Councils found that although there was still a crying need for houses for young families, a growing proportion of their existing housing stock was occupied by retired couples or, in some cases, by just one remaining member of a family, who no longer really needed family-type accommodation. This led to the development of a new type of local authority dwelling, specially designed for older people. Such accommodation is generally called sheltered housing. This usually takes the form of a number of small living units: bedroom, living room, kitchenette and bathroom, clustered around communal rooms which residents may use if they feel inclined. In most such schemes, a flat or unit is provided for a resident warden, who is available to help in case of difficulty, and can be called through a buzzer system linked to all units. In some of the more modern schemes, the Council also provides one or two guest bedrooms. In this way, by prior arrangement with the warden, residents can invite a friend or relative to visit them for a while without inconvenience. In these schemes, too, residents can live entirely separate lives, or join in the communal activities available, as they wish. The point about all these schemes is that even if the residents do lead completely independent lives, they have the assurance that companionship and support is always there if they need it. Many local authorities have sheltered housing of this type, but there is not yet enough of it to go round.

Your local Council may well operate a housing advisory service and be able to tell you what accommodation may become available in your area.

Housing associations

Apart from local government council house schemes, there are many housing associations providing accommodation to rent. The housing department of the local authority can give you details of any associations in your area. Directories of regional registered housing associations can be obtained free from The Housing Corporation. Another useful source of information is the National Federation of Housing Societies.

If you look in your telephone book you may well find that some of the bigger associations operate in your area. These include the Abbeyfield Society, Anchor Housing Association, Church Army Housing and the Royal British Legion. The Abbeyfield Society has over 600 houses throughout the country. Normally each house has up to 10 residents. The rooms are unfurnished, allowing residents to keep some of their treasured belongings. Send a stamped addressed envelope to the head office to obtain details.

Your local branch of Age Concern (old people's welfare organisation) will certainly be able to tell you of housing associations in your area and, indeed, has a special link with the Hanover Housing Association.

Points to remember

1. Specially designed retirement homes and sheltered housing schemes can offer many advantages for retired people.
2. These schemes allow independent living, in the knowledge that communal facilities, companionship and help are at hand whenever needed.

Chapter 10

Whose Responsibility?

A recognised need

The need for adequate preparation for retirement has become widely recognised during the past 25 years. At first, a few concerned people, observing the adverse effect which retirement could have upon people's lives, realised the value of preparation for this major new phase of life, and did their best to encourage it. Now there is general support for the idea.

Government ministers and departments, employers, trade unions, the medical profession, educationists, and representatives of voluntary services, have all affirmed their belief in the benefits which proper preparation can bring to people approaching retirement. The question is: What are these authorities really doing about it and whose responsibility is it to provide this guidance and the information which they all agree is necessary at that crucial time in a person's life? Unfortunately each authority tends to look to the other, although each has a share in this responsibility. There is little attempt at co-ordination among the various agencies concerned. The result is that the provision of advisory courses and other forms of retirement guidance, together with counselling in the UK, is haphazard in nature and in some areas entirely absent.

The individual

Some independently-minded people assert that individuals approaching retirement age should be sufficiently experienced in life to be able to cope with retirement when it comes. In their view, if preparation is required at all, then it is the individual's own responsibility. This attitude ignores the fact that most people about to retire have become accustomed over the years to look to their employer and to the Welfare State for guidance and information. Of course, there is individual responsibility, and so participation in any advisory course must be voluntary. Sadly, however, the people most likely to need guidance and help in retirement are those least likely to appreciate the need for preparation, or to be easily persuaded to do anything about it. Those in most need are also likely to be the least articulate about it.

But even if an employee, without any prompting, vaguely understands the need to be prepared in all the various aspects discussed in this book, how should he or she set about it without guidance and support?

The government

So far, little practical financial support has been given by government for the furtherance of pre-retirement education in the UK. However, the government has recently published a discussion document on elderly people in our society, entitled *A Happier Old Age*. This points out that just over £10,000 million, or a third of the total public expenditure on the main social programmes, is attributable to elderly people. Much of this goes on pensions. But within the health and personal social services, the average cost of care and treatment of a person aged over 75 is seven times that of a person of working age. In recognising that maintenance of good health in old age is important, the document states that

'much depends upon life style and the ability to adjust to changing circumstances including isolation and loss; but there are many simple things which can be done effectively to promote an enjoyable old age as well as prevent ill health . . . In essence this is the encouragement of physical, social and mental activity, and of measures designed to help prevent the development or worsening of handicapping conditions and to cope with disability.'

The document asks: 'How might these aims be best pursued?' In a paragraph referring to preparation for retirement, the document accepts that 'there is clearly much value in proper preparation.' It asks 'What kind of help and advice is needed to assist people in making this important change in their lives and in developing the right mental attitude to retirement?

How can families be helped to prepare for the changes and new opportunities — and in most cases the fall in income — that follows the retirement of the breadwinner?' The government invited comments on the discussion document by the end of October 1978. We are sure they will have received many constructive suggestions.

In November 1977, following the report of the special Council of Europe Working Party on preparation for retirement, the Committee of Ministers adopted the following Resolution, which recommends:

'That governments of member states take, or where appropriate encourage, the following measures:

(a) GENERAL PRINCIPLES
Adequate structures should be established in order to ease the transition from paid employment to the retirement years, so that people should be able to lead a socially useful life and derive personal satisfaction in retirement.

These structures should include, according to the conditions of the member state:

   (i) provisions for the necessary preparation for retirement, and
  (ii) facilities which will allow the retired person to take advantage of the opportunities which society offers him, eg in the education and cultural field.

(b) SPECIFIC MEASURES
1. Adequate facilities for preparation for retirement should be made available in such a way that all individuals:

   (i) be allowed sufficient time to make the necessary adjustment before entering into retirement;
  (ii) be given up-to-date information in areas such as finance, health, housing, legal matters and leisure to enable them to make their own personal arrangements;
 (iii) be enabled to continue and develop interests and activities which will help them to adapt smoothly to their new role in society;
  (iv) be encouraged to participate to the fullest in society through voluntary and paid activities, insofar as this is feasible and beneficial to society at large;
   (v) be encouraged as far as possible to lead healthy and

147

active lives;

(vi) be encouraged to view their new role as one which is contributing positively to the functioning of society.

2. Pre-retirement programmes should be conducted in accordance with the best principles of adult education, give recognition to the experience and the background of the participants, make provision for the participation of spouses, and at a minimum include:

☐ development of positive attitudes towards retirement,
☐ factual and positive information and advice on health during later life;
☐ general information and personal counselling on financial matters, information on housing alternatives and living arrangements;
☐ appropriate legal advice, information on social welfare, and other entitlements;
☐ information on leisure pursuits, cultural and sport opportunities, information on voluntary work activity and part-time employment, discussion of sociological factors.

3. Pre-retirement programmes should, ideally, take place five to ten years before retirement, and subsequently be reinforced by shorter programmes as the person nears the date of retirement, in order to take into account changes in particular areas.

4. Arrangements should be made, through national bodies or otherwise, for the development of policies concerning pre-retirement education and, where appropriate, the co-ordination of existing endeavours; due account should be taken of and support given to the contribution of voluntary bodies.

5. Such national bodies should be involved in the preparation and supply of information, literature and audio-visual material to organisers and tutors of pre-retirement programmes.

6. Adult education organisations and institutes should be encouraged to develop their contribution to the provision of pre-retirement education.

7. Employers and trade union organisations, farmers' associations and other relevant organisations should be invited to co-operate by providing realistic opportunities for as many as possible to participate in pre-retirement programmes.

8. Provision should be made for the training of sufficient personnel to act as tutors in these programmes; these tutors may be recruited from the areas of adult education and from people with particular expertise in the relevant fields.

(c) INFORMATION

1. Persons in spheres of influence in society, both in governmental and non-governmental positions, should be acquainted with the objectives, philosophy and method of pre-retirement education in order to gain their support.

2. Wide ranging and intensive publicity campaigns should be conducted to alert the general public and to develop an understanding of the need for pre-retirement education.

3. The mass media should be invited to co-operate in such campaigns.

4. Publicity should be organised on a continuing basis in order to bring about a more positive attitude by society towards retired people.

(d) RESEARCH

1. A concerted programme of research should be developed which would enable better insight to be obtained into the problems associated with retirement and which would provide a basis for a full understanding of the requirements involved in providing suitable pre-retirement training. The results of research should be collated and co-ordinated, and this information should be made freely available to pre-retirement educationists. Research institutes and universities should be asked to assist in the work of research.

2. Research in major interest areas should be sponsored and co-ordinated to avoid wasteful duplication.

3. A positive evaluation of the results of this research, particularly of its contribution to pre-retirement education, should be made periodically; the knowledge which tutors get from close contact with the people participating in

pre-retirement education should be used to ensure the
relevance of proposed research.

Governments of member states are invited to inform the
Secretariat General of the Council of Europe every five years
of the development in the implementation of the present
Resolution.'

We hope that this Resolution will yet prove to be the spur
for practical support by the government for the expansion of
pre-retirement education in this country. We are also
convinced that through proper preparation, many thousands
of people now approaching retirement would find it easier to
adapt to the new way of life; to find a new sense of purpose
and fresh opportunities; and to prolong their good physical
and emotional health and personal independence. We know of
no statistics, financial or otherwise, which might indicate the
proportion of elderly people who have become prematurely
dependent upon the health and personal social services
through lack of opportunity for preparing themselves for
retirement, but we are sure that the consequent mistakes
made and the frustrations and boredom felt by many people
on and after their retirement are factors which cannot be
ignored.

Employers

A number of the larger employers in the UK do in fact make
facilities available for their employees to obtain pre-retirement
training. This is provided in various ways and, as we indicate
in the next chapter, usually depends upon the nature of the
business concerned. While we are right to look to government
to give a strong lead, there is no doubt that the direct
relationship between employer and employee offers the most
practical means of securing pre-retirement education. Many
progressive employers now recognise this moral responsibility
for their older workers. Practical help given to staff in
preparing for retirement is often reflected in improved staff
relations which in turn redounds to the credit of the company,
and enhances its reputation as a good employer. Some large
companies have pioneered phased retirement schemes, in
which employees work a progressively shorter working week
during the last year or so of their employment. In the case of

managerial and executive posts, such a scheme provides a valuable transitional period which enables the company to implement a management succession programme, allowing a replacement to be eased in gradually, with the minimum of trouble or friction. That is an incidental benefit. Principally, these schemes are invaluable in helping the employee to make a gradual approach to retirement rather than having to take the sudden leap over the precipice from full-time work to full-time retirement. This gradual tapering off gives the employee time to adjust to the prospect of retirement and to become accustomed to having more leisure time at home. The employee's family and friends also have time in which to adjust to the new situation.

Some large organisations have introduced pensioner-visiting schemes. Examples are Unilever, Ford, Esso, John Lewis, the Civil Service and the Greater London Council.

In *Choice* magazine, Del Pasterfield, Supervisor, Welfare and Benefits Employee Programmes at Ford Motor Company Limited, has described the Ford scheme, which started in the early 1960s when Ford had fewer than 1,000 pensioners as compared with 11,000 today. Mr Pasterfield explained that at that early stage:

'Many pensioners were writing to us about matters unconnected with pensions and some wrote for no apparent reason at all. Many problems of loneliness, ill-adjustment and ill-health came to our notice. So, at much the same time, we took our first two tentative steps — the introduction of pre-retirement courses and a post-retirement contact scheme.'

This led to the establishment of the Ford Pensioners' Association. The company enlisted the help of 12 hand-picked pensioners as visitors, and launched a pilot scheme in the Essex area. Describing the scheme, Mr Pasterfield commented:

'From the start it seemed important to keep it simple, to develop a scheme which would be easy to run and which could grow without becoming administratively cumbersome. Each visitor was provided with a list of pensioners in his location, and sufficient stationery to organise his visiting. It was arranged that all reasonable out-of-pocket expenses would be reimbursed. The scheme was successfully received, and has now developed to the extent that we now have over 150 visitors reaching out to our pensioners throughout Britain. They meet with us at an annual conference to discuss Ford news and results and ideas for future progress . . . In addition we publish a regular Newsletter to include all current information about pensions, facilities and so on.'

In the course of visiting, vigorous efforts by the visitors have led to old friends rediscovering each other. Advice and help are offered, particularly to the very old, lonely, sick, disabled and housebound and the company is able to take up any special problems that arise.

In 1948, H M Stationery Office published a book by Sir Ernest Gowers, entitled *Plain Words — A Guide to the Use of English.* In a chapter on the choice of words, he quoted from one of *The Times* leading columns commenting upon the introduction of the word 'personnel' into the English language.

'Personnel, though in theory they are men and women, have only to be called personnel to lose their full status as human beings. They do not go, they proceed. They do not have, they are (or more often are not) in possession of. They do not ask, they make application for. Their minds, insofar as they may be deemed to have minds, are stocked not with the glories of knowledge, but with irrelevant and unmemorable statistics, such as their father's nationality at birth and the date on which they were last inoculated against yellow fever. Once they either kept things or gave them up; now they must retain or surrender them. Want (it is true) they do not know, nor need; but deficiencies and requirements are just as inconvenient. They cannot eat, they can only consume; they perform ablutions; instead of homes they have place(s) of residence in which, instead of living, they are domiciled. They are not cattle, they are not cyphers, they certainly are not human beings; they are personnel.'

Sir Ernest Gowers was advocating the use of plain words. We are sure that the vast majority of personnel managers today are very much involved in the welfare of the employees in their care, but there are still managements for whom 'personnel' is a convenient word absolving them from any feeling of moral responsibility for the well-being of employees once they have retired.

Lack of effective communication between employer and employed may also be a problem. We have known companies which decided to introduce pre-retirement courses for older employees, only to find a marked lack of enthusiasm among staff invited to attend. One reason is the reluctance of older employees to entertain any thought of retirement — they are unwilling to face it and react against a formal note asking them to attend a course which is the first positive step towards the reality of retirement. Another reason is suspicion: what is behind it? Redundancies? Early retirement? These fears and objections could largely be avoided if management would realise the overriding need for full consultation and joint planning on this sensitive issue, before courses are introduced.

Employers' organisations, such as the Confederation of British Industry and the British Institute of Management, support the idea of pre-retirement training and do, from time to time, draw the attention of employers and management to the ways in which it can benefit older employees.

The Training Services Division

The Training Services Division is a part of the Manpower Services Commission, and operates the Training Opportunities Scheme (TOPS). This offers free training, with pay, to men and women who want to develop their skills in order to improve their job prospects. It runs over 50 'Skillcentres' throughout the country and also provides training through colleges and private firms. Courses range from industrial and office courses to management and professional courses. Pre-retirement education would gain considerable impetus if it were to be recognised by the Training Services Division and the Commission. In present circumstances the Division will not accept such training as a proper charge on TSD funds. They consider themselves restricted by statute to the field of training for employment — not for leaving it! Perhaps employers' organisations and trade unions could use their influence to persuade the government to amend the law in this respect, so as to widen the scope of the Commission, the Division and the various Training Boards, to include pre-retirement training. We later mention the enlightened policy of the French government which positively supports and subsidises the concept of pre-retirement training as an integral part of 'l'éducation permanente' — life-long education.

Trade unions

As the General Secretary of the Trades Union Congress has pointed out to all affiliated organisations, the TUC regards it as important that educational facilities should be developed to ensure that work-people are provided with the opportunity and facilities to prepare themselves for retirement during the latter period of their employment. In drawing the attention of unions to the provisions which are already made by some

153

firms, Len Murray, General Secretary, has stated that, 'The TUC regards it as important that, where appropriate, trade unions should promote discussions with employers about establishing or improving arrangements for pre-retirement preparation for their members.'

In a recent interview recorded for *Choice* magazine, Mr Murray said:

'I would like to see a society in which retirement is regarded as a liberation, as an incentive to live actively and positively, to do things which you have always wanted to but have never found the time. So not only is there a need for improvements in income support but a need for a fundamental change in attitudes: change in the attitudes of a the individuals themselves and a change in the attitudes of families.'

He agreed that in recent years industry has made major progress in retirement planning, but went on to say:

'But industry is still not doing enough; I mean both sides of industry, neither the employers nor the unions. I would like to see unions more actively negotiating with employers to provide pre-retirement schemes and, with employers, bringing pressure to bear on local authorities to provide instruction and courses, to expose to the older section of the population the alternatives to work; to widen their ranges of choice which, too often, they do not see as choices at all but only as stark alternatives to having no job.'

Some unions do give active support, and collaborate fully with employers in the provision of training facilities for union members nearing retirement. This can do much to allay any fears of redundancy or enforced early retirement. Local union officials and shop stewards can do much to encourage employees to attend any courses provided. Sadly, however, some unions pay only lip service to the idea. Their energies are fully channelled into more pressing matters — wage claims, pay differentials, overtime payments, and similar questions of concern to their active membership. Retired members usually have little influence. If *all* unions were to realise the need, and would press for adequate facilities for pre-retirement training for their older members, they would do much to earn the gratitude of their retired members.

The voluntary services

PRE-RETIREMENT ASSOCIATION
The National Old People's Welfare Council, now more widely

known as Age Concern, pioneered the movement in 1955 by setting up a Preparation for Retirement study group. The work of this group led in turn to the formation of a Committee which included representatives of government departments, both sides of industry, educational, medical and welfare services and statutory and voluntary bodies. By 1964, there was sufficient enthusiasm to enable the Committee to become established as an independent charitable organisation known as The Pre-Retirement Association. Its membership is now well over 1,000 and includes some of the largest employers in the country. A number of local or regional associations have been established and affiliated to the national body. Most local pre-retirement associations run courses, and look to the national PRA as a co-ordinating body, providing information and resource material.

The Association itself runs one-day seminars and group counselling courses for client companies, and arranges conferences and courses from time to time for people actively involved in pre-retirement education.

It has introduced a retirement kit, containing various books and leaflets, and its book list contains a selection of relevant publications. It is also closely linked with the retirement planning magazine *Choice*.

The Association's supporting and co-ordinating functions; its ability to provide adequate resource material for course organisers and tutors; and its role in initiating relevant research, have been severely limited throughout its life by lack of funds, but as the only national organisation solely concerned with preparation for retirement it has a wealth of experience and a promising potential, given more practical support by the government.

AGE CONCERN

Age Concern England is a registered charity founded in 1940 to promote the welfare of elderly people. It acts as headquarters for 1,100 local groups throughout Britain who work with volunteers to provide visiting for the lonely, day centres, lunch clubs, transport schemes and many other services. Nationally, Age Concern provides a comprehensive information service and a wide range of publications. It supports local Age Concern organisers with a team of field officers and a training department. It also advises the government on legislation affecting the elderly, and campaigns on behalf of all elderly people.

Age Concern recognises that the increasing number of very elderly people in our society will mean inevitably an increased measure of support for them, and this will be reflected in both branches of the movement's work. More services will have to come from within the community (from families and voluntary bodies like Age Concern) as statutory bodies find themselves unable to meet growing needs. Age Concern believes that campaigns for improved pensions, housing and medical care should receive long-term planning, based on the implications of the population trends. It is closely linked with its sister organisations in Scotland, Wales and Northern Ireland.

HELP THE AGED

Help the Aged exists to make old age a time of active happiness. Founded in 1962, it promotes the welfare of the elderly both in Britain and overseas.

Its first work in Britain was the provision of sheltered housing for the aged, setting up pioneer housing associations, of which the largest is now Anchor Housing Association. In this way more than 7,000 flats have been provided. In a new venture, owners of under-occupied dwellings are invited to donate their houses for adaptation as flats for the elderly, the donor retaining one flat, rent free for life.

Help the Aged funds day centres and employment fellowship centres. Minibuses are provided for transport. Important medical research projects are being supported and work has started on rehabilitation units specifically for the aged, incorporating the latest advances in therapy.

Its education department prepares materials for schools. The charity produces its own monthly newspaper for the elderly in Britain: *Yours*. In running such a programme, Help the Aged depends considerably on the help of an army of willing volunteers, many of them retired people, engaged in fund raising and assisting in the administration of the movement.

THE WOMEN'S ROYAL VOLUNTARY SERVICE

The WRVS is also much involved in helping elderly and handicapped people. Its Meals on Wheels service is a splendid example of voluntary effort. Over the years, many thousands of housebound elderly people have had cause to be thankful for the arrival of the Meals on Wheels van, with a cheerful volunteer bringing a cooked lunch to their table or bedside.

There are many other voluntary organisations involved in community support for old people, and the work of all these bodies will grow rather than diminish as the proportion of elderly people in the population increases still further.

The discussion document *A Happier Old Age* stated that:

'An important objective of the health and personal social services is to enable elderly people to maintain independent lives in the community for as long as possible. Health services are provided by the primary health care team (the general practitioner. district nurse, health visitor, and their supporting staff) and by dentists, opticians, pharmacists and chiropodists. Social services are provided by the area social services team which might include social workers, home helps, people delivering meals on wheels, mobility officers for the blind, advisers on technical aids and adaptations, and occupational therapists.'

All this represents a formidable array of support services for the elderly, provided by the state, and in recent years there has been considerable expansion in most of these services. Yet the work of voluntary organisations is an integral part of the picture. They play an important role in supplementing the services provided by the statutory bodies. They are able to meet needs and provide new services which are beyond the present scope of the statutory services. Voluntary organisations are also able to display greater flexibility and can give help of a more personal kind. This might vary from practical help with the garden to redecorating the home; the organisation of 'adopt-a-grannie' schemes, through which lonely old people are given the opportunity to share in the life of a family and become adoptive grandparents to the children; or even the organisation of simple visiting schemes to the home or the hospital, which can do much to offset loneliness and to give elderly people a sense of comfort and belonging.

We have already described the work of Age Concern and the network of groups which it has built up throughout the country. The personal contacts which Age Concern's voluntary helpers establish with elderly people give them the opportunity to act in a co-ordinating role. The voluntary helper sees at first hand and identifies the type of assistance that an elderly person needs, and knows where that help can be obtained. This co-ordinating role flourishes, whatever the voluntary organisation concerned, where voluntary helpers come into personal contact with old people. Over a million people entitled to supplementary benefit do not apply. How many elderly people, caught in the poverty trap, struggle on in loneliness and in need because they do not know that it *is* available, or do not know how to apply for it? In these circumstances, a visit by a voluntary worker with a knowledge of the facilities available can be invaluable.

In chapter 7 we drew attention to the opportunities for voluntary work, and the scope in many spheres of community work, apart from that of help and care for the elderly. Retired people, particularly those who are recently retired, have a tremendous amount to offer the voluntary services in terms of skill and experience, coupled with the time available in which to provide it.

The adult education service

In our chapter on leisure, we described the wide range of courses available for retired people through the colleges and institutes of adult education. We also referred to the extra-mural courses run by universities, the specialised courses provided at residential colleges, and field study centres. If we could look at the overall picture in the UK, we would see that courses are provided on a tremendous variety of subjects; that such courses may range from single or two-day courses and short residential courses, to courses spread over three or more terms; and that courses are provided in places ranging from modern liberal arts colleges offering a continuous and varied programme of day and evening courses, to village halls and schools where evening classes are held on one or two evenings each week. In all, there are hundreds of places, spread throughout the country, at which adult education of one type or another is being provided.

On the whole, these centres respond to public demand. If the local further education officer finds that there is a firm demand for a course on a particular subject, and a dozen or more people are likely to take part, the likelihood is that the course will be provided. This is the pattern which emerges from time to time so far as pre-retirement advisory courses are concerned. The demand for an advisory course usually comes from the personnel manager or the welfare officer of a local firm which has a number of employees nearing retirement age. If a regular series of courses can be established, with the continuing support of the larger employing organisations in the area, pre-retirement advisory courses can become a permanent feature of the adult education programme. More often than not the time comes when the company whose employees form the majority of the class finds that there are very few staff due to attend a course in the coming year. The danger then is that the course will be cancelled through lack of support. We have seen this happen time and time again. We have also observed that the places where pre-retirement training is a flourishing and permanent feature of the adult education programme are those where a pre-retirement or retirement association has been formed. The association carries out an organising and co-ordinating role, providing a much-needed link between the adult education service and representatives of commerce, industry, and other employing organisations in its area. Often, the association's governing body includes representatives of local and central government, the churches, and the voluntary organisations operating in the area. Advisory courses provided by the adult education service usually take the form of six or more full-day or half-day sessions spread over an equivalent number of weeks, so that the people attending have ample opportunity for group discussions and questions, and course organisers and tutors have time to help those attending, not only by giving them factual information but by helping them to appreciate the need for an adjustment in mental attitudes and the value of a positive approach to their coming retirement.

Apart from courses organised directly by local education authorities, a wide range of courses is provided by the Workers' Educational Association (WEA), including pre-retirement advisory courses in some areas. The WEA's contribution to adult education is made in conjunction with the universities and local education authorities. This Association is unique in form as a national voluntary body made up of its students, individual subscribers and affiliated organisations. It has no party political or sectarian ties, and its courses are open to all adults.

159

Universities and retirement education

An encouraging new development is the increasingly active interest being taken by some of the universities in pre-retirement education. Keele University, for instance, is closely associated with proposals for carrying out studies which could show positive evidence of the benefits of pre-retirement education and also examining the relative merits of different types of courses. The University of Surrey is also taking a lead in the field of pre and post-retirement education. An associate lectureship has recently been established for the purpose of developing pre-retirement education, and a King's Fund research fellowship established in the University which will investigate the types of problems found among retired Health Service staff.

We hope that in time other universities will follow this initiative and assume a more active role by helping to co-ordinate and develop facilities for pre-retirement education within their respective counties; by initiating and encouraging further research into the problems of retirement; and by providing the specialised training and guidance needed by tutors, organisers and counsellors involved in this particular sphere of adult education.

Points to remember

1. The need for retirement education is recognised, but the responsibility for its provision is not accepted. Practical support is needed from the government, employers, and trade unions.
2. Demands on voluntary organisations will increase with the ageing population.
3. More local retirement associations should be set up to co-ordinate pre-retirement training with the adult education movement.
4. Universities have a vital role to play in the future of retirement education.

Chapter 11
Resources and Courses

Where can you obtain advice and information about
retirement? This chapter tries to answer the question from
two points of view. First, for the man or woman nearing
retirement, or already retired; secondly for the employers
(and union representatives) who wish to discover the best
ways and means of helping older employees to prepare for
retirement.

The individual's needs

For people who have to do all this for themselves, either
because they are self-employed, or because their employer
has no apparent interest in their welfare after retirement,
there is a list of useful addresses at the end of this book,
through which can be obtained useful advice and
information on all aspects of retirement. If this applies to
you, do not hesitate to ask. But please remember that many
voluntary bodies are short of funds, and will appreciate the
courtesy of a stamped addressed envelope for a reply. There
may be an adult education or Workers' Educational
Association retirement course which you can attend in your
area. Better still, you may find that there is a local pre-
retirement or retirement association nearby where you can
obtain expert guidance and details of their courses. At
present there are associations in Basildon, Bedford, Berkshire,
Bristol, Coventry, Croydon, Cumbria, Essex, Glasgow,
Greater London, Greater Manchester, Gwent, Merseyside,
Nottingham, Northern Ireland, Rugby, St Helens, Sheffield,
Shropshire, South Glamorgan, Southampton,
Staffordshire, Walsall and Wolverhampton.
  The Pre-Retirement Association can send you details, or

you can enquire at your local library or Council offices.

For reading material, apart from publications dealing with the subject in general, there are books related to particular aspects of it, such as finance, and health. The Pre-Retirement Association includes a number of such books in its book list. Also, the Association has used its skill and expertise to compile retirement kits. These contain books, pamphlets and relevant official information leaflets, dealing with income tax, retirement pensions, state benefits, national savings, safety in the home, and services available to the retired.

One very useful publication, both for the pre and post-retired is the monthly magazine *Choice*.

Choice magazine is the official voice of the Pre-Retirement Association and with a circulation approaching 80,000 copies a month is now one of the chief ways in which many people are introduced to the subject of planning for their retirement. Well over 2,000 companies buy the magazine to give to staff who are approaching or enjoying their retirements.

With regular articles on the main areas of planning: finance, health, housing, recreation, part-time jobs, holidays and mental attitudes, the magazine forms the first effective continuous guide to retirement planning.

Contributors include Dr H Beric Wright, MB, FRCS, President of the PRA, Deputy Chairman of the BUPA Medical Centre and Medical Adviser, Institute of Directors; Edward Eves, author of the book *Money and your Retirement*; and a host of other writers skilled in their subject.

Choice has recently added another useful reference work for those approaching retirement, called the *Retirement Briefing File*. The document is in loose leaf form with a wide range of factual information, especially on the financial aspects of retirement. The purchase price includes a year's updating service. If the Chancellor has a mini (or a major) budget which alters the figures, the affected sheets are reprinted and posted to purchasers.

The employer

Employers range in size from the multi-national company employing thousands of people, to the corner shopkeeper or local garage owner, employing one, two or three people at most. The great majority of businesses in the UK fall somewhere between the two extremes. There is also a tremendous diversity in the types of business. A multiple stores group will probably have a network of retail shops spread around the UK, each with a relatively small number of staff of whom a significant proportion will be short-term and part-time employees. Such an organisation will have a different approach to retirement training from that of a great manufacturing concern employing a large number of people in one place.

An employer with few employees will take a different view again. His organisation would probably be hard put to it to cope if a high proportion of his key staff were regularly absent, attending an extended pre-retirement advisory course.

The type and extent of the provision that an employer can make for staff will normally be determined by three factors:

(a) the size of the organisation in respect of the number of employees;
(b) the nature and profitability of the business;
(c) the facilities in the area and the resource material available.

Strangely, there are staunch advocates of one particular type of advisory course as opposed to another; people who fail to appreciate that the first two factors must be taken into account and that the practical limitations which these factors impose, from the employer's point of view, must be respected. Once an employer becomes convinced that some suitable form of pre-retirement training for the employees would be a worthwhile thing, a number of questions will arise about the facilities available. Management will probably issue an instruction to a senior member of staff: find out all about it and submit the recommendations. This order raises an inevitable question — who gets the instruction? In a large organisation it might be the welfare officer, the pensions manager, or the personnel officer. It all depends on the internal arrangements of the organisation concerned. Each may claim (or oppose any suggestion) that pre-retirement training should come within his province. This brings us back to our previous chapter: whose responsibility? The same problem sometimes arises in the firm, in that each officer tends to look to another with the result that nothing much is done.

However, let us assume that a senior member of staff has been given the responsibility of investigating the problem and submitting a report to management. We suggest that the outline of his or her enquiries might be:

1. Is there a local pre-retirement or retirement association in the area? If so, will this advise on facilities available and be able to make arrangements for employees to attend a suitable advisory course? If not —
2. Are advisory courses already available through the adult education services in the locality? If so, the education officer will no doubt be pleased to arrange for people to attend. Depending on there being sufficient numbers, this officer may be prepared to make adjustments in course times and dates to suit the employer. If there are no courses of this nature at present, the officer may be able to start them, given the promise of a sufficient number of employees committed to attend.
3. If nothing is available under 1 or 2, what else can be done? This alternative depends very much on the size of the organisation.

We have already mentioned the Pre-Retirement Association's retirement kits, book list of relevant publications and the monthly magazine *Choice*. The Association has also recently introduced a group counselling service, which is available for smaller companies. This service sends an expert, usually for a day, to speak to a small group and to discuss with them the various aspects of retirement which concern them.

Many larger organisations have facilities for in-company training. For client companies, the PRA will run a one or two-day seminar, which consists of a series of talks by experts on finance, health, part-time work, leisure activities, living arrangements and mental attitudes. Many companies now run their own advisory courses for staff, and find it convenient to bring them in to a central assembly point for the purpose. In-company courses normally deal (or should deal) with the six aspects included in the PRA seminar programme, and often include a talk by a company expert who explains the details of the staff pension scheme. A word of caution: the success of any advisory course depends on having an experienced course organiser in the chair and expert speakers to deal with specialised topics included in the programme. Here again, the PRA can offer guidance. They also maintain a list of experts available to run courses and to speak on the subjects involved.

In-company training may consist of one or two-day courses, residential weekend courses at the company's training centre, or one afternoon a week sessions spread over a number of weeks.

Much useful advice is contained in the PRA *Handbook for Course Organisers.*

A recent development, welcomed by many in the field of pre-retirement education, has been the production by the British Life Assurance Trust for Health Education (BLAT) of a series of multi-media packages dealing with retirement education. BLAT is a registered charity established by the British Medical Association, The Life Offices' Association and the Associated Scottish Life Offices, to promote innovations in health and medical education. The series, entitled *The Next Twenty Years*, consists of eight programmes, each having a cassette tape and 40 to 50 slides, together with a recording script and study booklets. An educational handbook is provided with each complete set, but the programmes can also be purchased separately. The cassette tapes have two tracks. Track No 1 has Richard Baker (BBC television newsreader and broadcaster) reading the advice of the experts (this track can be synchronised with the slides) and track No 2 (sound only) contains a dramatised account of pensioners' real experiences. BLAT has also provided an updating service, at minimum cost.

Dr Don Clarke, Director of BLAT, is firmly convinced of the value of audio-visual presentations in attracting interest and promoting learning. He points out that these programmes can be used:

1. By any experienced or inexperienced person who has access to a simple cassette tape-recorder and slide projector.
2. To act either as a supplement to existing speakers or to be used in their absence.
3. As a 'starter pack' to which local material, eg pensions

information, can be added or substituted.

4. But above all else as a trigger to discussion and debate about the problems we all encounter in retirement, and to which we need to take a positive attitude.

We have given you a brief review of the main options to be considered. In our experience, a company will often take only limited action to start with, perhaps by supplying employees nearing retirement with a PRA retirement kit or one of the books recommended by the PRA, or maybe by giving them a year's subscription to *Choice* magazine. In some cases a company will arrange for the PRA to run a one-day seminar for older employees and then go on to provide their own in-company training, developed and modified to suit their particular circumstances.

But whatever the size of the employing organisation and whatever the facilities (or lack of them) available in the locality, we do urge:

1. That all employers, even if they have only one or two staff nearing retirement, should make a positive decision *now* to do something practical to ensure that their employees have some means of preparing for their retirement.

2. That the providers, that is the organisations and individuals involved in retirement education and training, (whether voluntary bodies, educationists, or experts in specialised subjects such as health or finance), do all they can to increase the range and to improve the quality of the resource material at present available; to train both existing tutors and new ones in the proper use of educational techniques; and to accept the need for *flexibility* in course provision to meet the differing requirements of employing organisations.

Detailed advice on the arrangement and content of retirement advisory courses is beyond the scope of this book, but examples may prove a useful guide.

The following is typical of the type of programme for one of the Pre-Retirement Association's Industrial Advisory Service one-day seminars.

When the PRA conducts a seminar, it urges the client company to extend an invitation to the seminar to the husbands or wives of the employees attending. All participants are asked to complete a questionnaire at the end of the seminar, expressing their views of the seminar and the value to them of the individual talks. The replies (which remain anonymous) are later analysed and assessed for the client company. If necessary, adjustments may then be made in the programme for future seminars. Each member of staff attending receives a booklet, summarising the main points of the various talks given:

SEMINAR HELD IN CONJUNCTION WITH
THE PRE-RETIREMENT ASSOCIATION

Programme	Subject
9.00 am	Opening of the seminar
9.15 am	'Mental attitudes towards retirement'
10.00 am	Coffee
10.10 am	'Health in retirement'
11.00 am	'Jobs — paid and unpaid'
11.45 am	Tour of the company's premises
12.30 pm	Lunch
1.40 pm	'Pensioners' clubs'
1.50 pm	'What to do with your leisure'
2.35 pm	'Should you move to another house?'
3.15 pm	Tea and distribution of questionnaires
3.25 pm	'Financial planning'
4.15 pm	'State benefits'
5.00 pm	Summing up
5.05 pm	Dispersal

Many organisations provide their own in-company training. The following is an example of a two-day seminar provided by C & A Modes for members of the company's staff. The seminar included an audio-visual tape-slide presentation entitled *The Next Milestone,* and a film entitled *Time on Your Hands.*

C & A MODES PRE-RETIREMENT SEMINAR IN HOTEL

Subject	Time
Lunch in hotel	
1. Informal welcome with coffee after lunch (by Personnel Department)	2.00
2. Your company pension (by Pension Fund Manager)	2.30
3. *The Next Milestone Part I* — Film (including question session)	3.00
Tea	
4. *The Next Milestone Part II* — Film (including question session)	3.30
5. Help from the Citizens' Advice Bureau	4.00
Close of Day 1	5.00
Dinner in the hotel	7.30
6. Introduction to Day 2	9.00
7. State benefits for retirement (by Department of Health and Social Security)	9.15
8. Leisure: *Time on Your Hands* — Film	10.15
Coffee	
9. Health and safety in retirement (by a doctor)	10.45
10. Open Forum	
Lunch	11.45
Close	12.30

The following programme is an example of a weekend residential course, provided for staff by W H Smith & Son Limited at their staff training centre at Milton Hill, Berkshire. This programme also included an audio-visual presentation.

W H SMITH & SON LIMITED PRE-RETIREMENT SEMINAR PROGRAMME

Time	Subject
Friday	
1100 - 1230	Arrive Milton Hill
1230 - 1300	Reception
1300 - 1400	Lunch
1415 - 1430	Welcome and opening
1430 - 1445	Seminar briefing
1445 - 1515	*The Next Milestone* (film)
1515 - 1530	Tea
1530 - 1630	The challenge of retirement
1630 - 1730	Company pension scheme
1900	Dinner
2000 - 2100	Saga Holidays Ltd
2100 - 2300	Lounge bar
Saturday	
0800 - 0830	Breakfast
0900 - 1030	Managing your money
1030 - 1045	Coffee
1045 - 1115	Your personal insurances
1115 - 1230	Health in later years
1245 - 1400	Lunch
1400 - 1500	Social Security benefits
1500 - 1515	Tea
1515 - 1615	Leisure interests
1615 - 1715	Open forum
1715 - 1730	Seminar closure
1800 - 2300	Manor bar
1930	Dinner
Sunday	
0800 - 0830	Breakfast
0830 - 1000	Seminar disperses

The next example is a course programme for one of the
Morley College, London, Preparation for Retirement Courses,
held on one afternoon a week (2.15 - 4.30 pm) over a period
of 11 weeks. Morley College (address: 61 Westminster
Bridge Road, London SE1 7HT) is recognised as a pioneer in
the field of pre-retirement education and regularly runs as
many as 10 courses a year (including an evening one). There
is a continuing process of assessment and analysis of course
content and presentation, aimed at achieving the maximum
possible benefit for the participants. Many adult education
courses have been modelled on this example:

MORLEY COLLEGE COURSE PROGRAMME

Subjects to be covered include:

Session No

Introduction
1 *Welcome to course members and approach to
retirement. Pension schemes

Home and neighbourhood
2 (a) Location; neighbourhood resources
(b) Indoors, gardens; relationships
3 (c) Living alone
*(d) Discussion (home/neighbourhood/relationships)

The wherewithal
4 (a) Budgeting
(b) State pensions
5 (c) Taxation
(d) Taxation (ii) *or* concessions and rights
6 (e) Investment and other financial matters

2,000 hours plus
7 *(a) Leisure pursuits and holidays
8 (b) Opportunities to learn: an appetiser
(c) Diet and nutrition
9 (d) Supplementing income
(e) Helping voluntarily

The retired person complete
10 Keeping healthy
11 *(a) Adjustment
(b) Review of course

* *denotes group discussion will occupy part of the time.*

Finally, we give you two examples from overseas — the first is a typical programme for a course organised by the National Preparation for Retirement Council of Norway.

PRE-RETIREMENT COURSE

Seminar — 3 days — 11 topics

1st day
1000	Opening of the course
1015	The need for preparation for retirement
1200	Lunch
1400	The financial position
1600	Legal questions
1800	Dinner

2nd day
0900	The state of health
1030	The pensioner's rights
1200	Lunch
1400	Housing in old age
1600	The need for physical activity
1800	Dinner

3rd day
0900	Ageing and personality
1030	Diet and nutrition
1200	Conversation with 'experienced' pensioner
1300	Lunch
1400	The need for contact and solidarity
1600	Summing up
1800	Dinner

171

The second comes from the USA and is the programme for a
'Planning for retirement' workshop, organised in California
by the Trade Union Movement (The Labor Council).

The programme comprised six sessions held on a Saturday
morning from 10 am to noon. The workshop staff were
co-ordinated by a university lecturer and a representative
from the Teachers' Union, who was an expert on counselling
older workers. Each session was independent of the others.
The fee per session was three dollars and spouses were invited
to attend at no extra cost.

PLANNING FOR RETIREMENT WORKSHOP

1. *Financial planning:*
   Property — savings — investments — retirement budget —
   before and after — long-range planning — legal problems —
   where to get help and advice — pensions — benefits —
   social security.
2. *Planned health care and health maintenance:*
   Emotional health — keeping healthy — county health
   resources.
3. *Housing:*
   Keep your home or move? — ideal housing for the older
   person — adult communities.
4. *Employment:*
   Employment opportunities for people over 50 — a second
   career — job hunting techniques — county resources.
5. *Leisure:*
   Need to plan leisure — leisure day dreams — leisure
   reality — community involvement — skills and hobbies —
   travel — leisure resources in the county — adult education
   programmes.
6. *Opportunities of retirement:*
   Decision-making — meeting inflation — marriage and the
   family — boredom.

Points to remember

1. There are ways and means by which individuals nearing retirement can obtain information and advice for themselves.
2. Whether an employing organisation is large or small, it can offer its employees practical help in preparing for retirement. Some firms have also introduced phased retirement and pensioner visiting schemes.
3. There are various types of advisory courses, differing in length and content, but they can usually be tailored to suit the requirements of both employer and employee. Flexibility is essential.

Chapter 12
Retirement Round the World

When the authors were with the Pre-Retirement Association, visitors from many countries came to the headquarters to compare notes on pre-retirement training. In addition, the meetings of the Council of Europe Working Party on Preparation for Retirement in Strasbourg provided a forum for the exchange of views on data collected from the 19 nation membership of the Council.

We have selected interesting facets of educational work overseas in the hope that the exchange of ideas may hasten progress in an area where there is yet much to be achieved. We have not seen such an international summary in any other book on retirement.

Australia

Pioneer work in the Antipodes was instigated by the Early Planning for Retirement Association based in Melbourne. Because of the vast distances involved it has to date been difficult to set up a nationwide organisation.

A recent encouraging development is the initiative taken by the Workers' Education Association of South Australia. The WEA of South Australia was responsible for establishing the Pre-Retirement Association of South Australia but the PRA has its own independent Committee of Management. The WEA has been working in the field of adult education since 1917. The PRA is a voluntary organisation which attempts to recognise and cater for the needs of people who are planning their retirement, or who are already retired.

The PRA tells employers that retirement planning courses:
(a) boost staff morale, taking much of the uncertainty and insecurity out of impending retirement;

    (b) are tangible, low-cost indications of your interest in employee welfare;

    (c) project a good public image.

Courses are offered covering the topics of: health, finance, accommodation, personal adjustment, social security and law.

Bulgaria

Bulgaria is a member of the Communist bloc which is linked together in the organisation Comecon. One of the authors took the opportunity when on holiday to see at first hand pre-retirement provisions in a communist state. Regular staff meetings are held in all factories and offices, and lectures are given to staff approaching retirement on the usual topics, as in the UK; for example, on health and activities.

Emphasis is placed not only on what people might do after they retire, but also on their active participation in other activities before retirement. The Bulgarian pension expert was emphatic that under the socialistic scheme, Bulgarian pensioners do not dread the financial aspects of retirement since they know life is not going to be difficult. Social Security is entirely in the hands of the state and the co-operative organisations. During his or her working life, no Bulgarian has to contribute towards the pension he or she receives when he or she reaches the state retirement age, which is normally 55 for women and 60 for men.

Special efforts are made to show the workers how to deal with the necessary forms that pensioners have to complete before they retire so that when the time comes the workers will be confident about and fully conversant with their entitlements. This contrasts sharply with the UK where thousands of pensioners do not claim their supplementary benefits, rent allowances and rate rebates, and the government has to spend thousands of pounds on advertising to reach the public *after* they have retired.

On being asked if Bulgarians migrate from Sofia to the Black Sea on retirement, the reply came: 'In Bulgaria, the grandparents stay where their children are; they are the built-in baby sitters!'

Canada

There is an increasing interest in retirement planning in
Canada. Before the introduction of old-age pensions,
retirement for most people meant dire poverty. It is not
surprising that there was a deep-seated fear of retirement as
senior citizens knew they would be financially dependent on
their children and the uncertain benefits of the old welfare
system and private charity.

Happily, as the financial climate has improved, there has
been much evidence of healthy experimentation in the pre-
retirement planning field. Five main sections of the
community are already working in the movement, ie
companies, unions, government bodies, community groups
and educational institutions. Current evidence indicates a
growing tendency of cohesion between these bodies which
augurs well for the whole retirement planning movement.

A splendid example of how discussion material becomes
available is the Pre-Retirement Resource Kit produced by the
Ministry of Community and Social Services, Toronto, Ontario,
under the title of *Retirement — It's a Lifetime*. The kit
contains separate booklets dealing with: Housing; Legal issues;
Work after retirement; Consumer information; Physical
health; The individual and retirement; Toward an
understanding of retirement.

France

The French have long accepted the concept of the four ages
of man: learning, working, retirement and dependence.

French employers by law have to pay to the state a levy
calculated according to the amount of their total wages bill
to pay for the country's system of life-long education
(l'éducation permanente). The French Parliament has ruled
that pre-retirement training falls within the definition of
'vocational training as part of life-long education'. French
workers approaching retirement can now take training leave
to attend approved preparation for retirement courses, and
employers can deduct the cost involved from their obligatory
contribution. This has been a tremendous incentive
throughout France for the setting up of pre-retirement courses.

The Universities of the Third Age allow retired people,

irrespective of educational standards, to use all the facilities
of the University.

We have much to learn from our partners in the Common
Market. In the United Kingdom there is a great need to
provide a stable financial stimulus for retirement preparation.
In line with the French, we could increase the span of the
third age of life, and reduce the dependant period which
makes such heavy demands on the country's health and social
services as well as on charitable organisations.

Ireland

RETIREMENT PLANNING COUNCIL OF IRELAND

There is a growing interest in Ireland in the problems of
retirement and in retirement preparation. The establishment
of the Retirement Planning Council of Ireland resulted from
the voluntary spare-time work of people from different
organisations and backgrounds who recognised the need for
an effective agency to promote preparation for retirement in
the interests both of individuals and of the community.
The Dublin Institute of Adult Education pioneered pre-
retirement courses and the Rev Eoin Murphy (from the
Institute) was a member of the Council of Europe Working
Party.

The Retirement Planning Council has the support of
management, the trade unions, educational institutions and
the state services. It has established an advisory service, and
it assists in the running of courses. It helps to establish local
pre-retirement associations, and promotes research into
retirement attitudes and problems.

Although the number of pre-retirement courses is
increasing, at present they cover only a small proportion
of the population, and much remains to be done.

Most of the courses established so far are in Dublin; there
are very few courses in other parts of the country. The
Retirement Planning Council has therefore embarked on a
programme of seminars in provincial centres. Enquiries to:
The Director, Retirement Planning Council of Ireland,
59 Lansdowne Road, Dublin 4.

Japan

In Japan, the age of retirement can be as low as 50 years or as high as 70 years according to one's employer. Once a worker has retired, he is sheltered by the close and protective family group.

As in the Western world, so in the East. The extended family system is under attack, but in Japan it has not yet crumbled away completely. Most people still believe that the onus of looking after the elderly rests with the grown-up children of the family and not with the state. The comparatively early retirement age, and the increasing life span has, however, encouraged many older persons to continue working in a different field after their main career has ended. Large companies allow employees to retire, paying them an annuity and then engaging them for less demanding work. Retraining schemes allow pensioners to acquire new skills, such as cultivation of the world-famous Japanese 'Bonsai' miniature trees. The health of pensioners is safeguarded by regular medical examinations. Although formal pre-retirement training is still in an embryonic stage, the Japanese way of life generally cushions the pensioner against the problems of loneliness and lack of purpose on reaching retirement age.

Norway

The National Preparation for Retirement Council is a semi-public body which obtains substantial support from the Ministry of Social Affairs. Representation on the Council includes the Employers' Federation, the trade unions and friendly societies as well as government ministries. Insurance companies have shown initiative in the provision of films and audio-visual material.

The main functions of the Council are to:

1. Train course leaders.
2. Arrange/co-ordinate preparation for retirement programmes.
3. Ensure contact with mass media.
4. Publish pamphlets.
5. Provide audio-visual material.
6. Promote research.

Experience has proved that simple pamphlets with humorous cartoons produced a considerable impact on those who lacked the reading habit. These are the people with the greatest need.

Norway made a valuable contribution to the field of pre-retirement training by hosting an international conference in 1977. Jan Atle Andersen, Head of Secretariat, the Norwegian Joint Committee on Preparation for Retirement, was Vice-Chairman of the Council of Europe Working Party on Preparation for Retirement.

South Africa

In 1966, following a conference attended by overseas experts, a steering committee representative of industry, commerce, education, and medical and social services, was set up to investigate ways and means of helping South Africans to prepare for retirement. In 1967, the Witwatersrand Retirement Council was formed. Its subsequent success led to the establishment of branches in a number of other centres, and eventually to the entire organisation being re-named The Retirement Association. It now comprises some 70 companies and groups, and member companies can nominate employees to attend the Association's 'Design for Living' courses, initially 15 years, then 10, five and two years before retirement. The courses cover: mental and physical health, nutrition, development of the mental potential, extension of interests into the arts and sciences, finance in all its aspects, the need for continued education, a place to live, an occupation (gainful or otherwise), and travel.

The Association also runs an employment bureau which is free for those over the age of 60. Among other services, it has an advisory bureau and runs a continuity club to represent the interests of South Africans around retirement age.

The Association believes that its first duty to the people it serves 'is to promote health consciousness; the awareness that the knowledge, wisdom and experience, accumulated over a lifetime, can best be utilised for the benefit of the individual and the community by the retention, and application, of one's mental and physical faculties'.

Spain

PREPARACIÓN A LA JUBILACIÓN!

Two Spanish doctors, Martinez Gomez and Salgado Alba, presented a paper on preparation for retirement to a Belgrade Congress organised by the Eurag organisation. Eurag is a non-profit-making body which was founded in 1962 with the aim of defending the interests of the elderly throughout Europe.

The two doctors believed that the transition from active professional life to life in retirement was one of the biggest problems of modern industrial society, since it brought a host of difficulties, economic, social, professional and personal, to the individuals concerned. They saw that retirement demanded a capacity for adaptation, but this came at a time of life when that capability was considerably reduced.

In Spain, these doctors were devising programmes aimed at action and based on experience. The goal of the programmes was the removal of negative attitudes, and the awakening of the participants' desire to gain knowledge about new aspects of living so that life could be lived to the full. The doctors asserted that advice should be given on financial problems, housing, social integration including leisure interests, health including hygiene and nutrition, and further education.

Perhaps we in Britain can learn most from the Spanish phrase *preparación a la jubilación* (preparation for joy). The very sound of the words inspires excitement and challenge, which contrasts sharply with our own more prosaic expression of 'preparation for retirement'.

Switzerland

The central organisation for the co-ordination of pre-retirement training is the Swiss foundation Pro Senectute based in Zurich. It does not organise courses itself but co-operates with employers, trade unions, churches, local government and adult education organisations in the promotion of courses.

Courses organised can vary in length from six hours to 90 hours. One programme has been devised to cover a five-day vacation period. Between 1968 and 1974, 95 courses took place. Approximately half of these were held during working hours, without loss of pay. One sample course, for participants between the ages of 46 and 60, involved the use of group discussions and films on the themes: how not to get old; contacts and bonds; involvement; humanisation of work; new opportunities for the couple; enjoying leisure.

On the last evening, the course organisers, a theatre troupe and musicians, collaborated to produce a cabaret on the highlights of the course. The music and dancing on this last informal occasion brought the course to a successful conclusion.

Miss Julie Winter of Pro Senectute brought a wealth of practical experience to the meetings of the Council of Europe Working Party.

USA

ACTION FOR INDEPENDENT MATURITY

The American Association of Retired Persons claims to be the world's largest and most active organisation devoted to helping retired people to pack the greatest enjoyment into their lives. With a membership of more than seven million, the AARP and its affiliated associations have considerable financial resources. These are used to maintain a vociferous political lobby in Washington to protect the rights and privileges of senior citizens.

The AARP found that many problems which arise in retirement would never have happened if proper planning had preceded retirement. With this in mind, it founded AIM (Action for Independent Maturity) to help future retirement generations to enjoy retirement. Membership is open to those between 50 and 65. Members receive the bi-monthly magazine *Dynamic Maturity*. Its articles cover all aspects of pre-retirement living, offering advice on legal matters, leisure activities, retirement locations and housing, second careers and finance. In the absence of a National Health Service, health matters are a major worry for America's senior citizens. AIM offers, at discount prices, a postal service for medicines and a Group Health Insurance Plan. Other services include a travel bureau, and car and life insurance.

In answering the question whether 50 is too early to start pre-retirement planning, AIM says that by then most people find their family responsibilities easing; they begin to think about achieving all their ambitions which were long postponed because of family commitments. From 50 onwards, the transitional period begins — the time to move into a way of life which will provide for your own happiness and comforts.

The older generation in the USA are far more politically sensitive than their British cousins. They have noted the success of the youngsters who campaigned successfully for the withdrawal from Vietnam. They are the survivors of the great depression in America of the 1930s. From the respectability of the base provided by the AARP has sprung a coalition of active workers who call themselves the Gray Panthers. They are fighting positively to make people realise that 'those of us over 65 are just like people under 65. We have the same needs for housing, adequate medical care, financial security, sex: there's nothing different about us'.

Comment on USA employers from *Choice* magazine: 'Hundreds of companies offer a comprehensive programme of pre-retirement counselling. Why all this concern for employees who will soon leave the payroll? It is good business'.

Conclusions

We have tried to be completely factual in describing the retirement situation in this country. Only in chapter 12 (Retirement Round the World), where we have described the situation in other countries ranging from the Western world to the Communist bloc, have we expressed an occasional criticism of the UK.

At the end of each chapter we are left with the nagging thought that so much still remains to be done for our seniors. There is a basic state pension which is by European standards woefully inadequate. The new scheme launched in 1977 will take 20 years to come to fruition. Are we to wait patiently for two decades while *each year* a new host of 1,500,000 pensioners receive their pension books? The Government's Job Release scheme publicised extensively to tempt seniors to take early retirement has failed. Why? Briefly, the answer is that most workers are perturbed by the implications of retirement. The country has not created, as yet, the right conditions to induce older workers to leave happily the cocoon provided for them by the employers and the government. Collectively, the workers are a force to be reckoned with — they represent 21,000,000 voters. People listen to the voice of the TUC although it boasts only 9,000,000 members.

United Kingdom, wake up! Your pensioners also total 9,000,000. That is 9,000,000 votes!

Many politicians pay only lip service to this potential voting strength at election times because pensioners are not organised. They are not vociferous and, generally speaking, are apathetic. We can learn something from the United States. The respectable American Association of Retired Persons, with a 7,000,000 membership, has produced a loosely knit pressure group with the vivid title of Gray Panthers. These are the mature militants. They urge older people who are interested in social change, first, to work to take care of their own needs and then, transcending this, to help the elderly poor. Older people have been forced to become politically active because of the fear that they will not be able to live out the rest of their lives with dignity. Why do we accept in the UK that retirement must be synonymous with a fall in income and thus, living standards? Give our seniors adequate pensions, with some flexibility in the retirement age, linked with eligibility for state pension; and give employers financial incentives to mount pre-retirement courses, and to offer personal counselling services. The fears of retirement could be banished within a few years. Seniors might then be prepared to retire in advance of the present statutory pension ages. As a consequence, the figure of one-and-a-half million unemployed would be drastically reduced.

The central machine to be used? In its present form, the Pre-Retirement Association does not have the capability. It receives no regular financial support from government and as a registered charity it cannot act effectively as a pressure group. The average grant of £14,000 for three years received by the PRA from 1974 to 1977 was subsequently reduced. Even at the rate of £14,000 per annum the government grant worked out at less than three pence per head for every person reaching retiring age.

Employers need to be reminded that pre-retirement services are good for business and for their image. Trade unionists must not be solely concerned with the size of the pay packet, but must also look at the size of the pension – the retirement pay packet.

The government should implement the recommendations of the Council of Europe Working Party on Preparation for Retirement which have been endorsed at ministerial level. To bring them into force, the government must set up a new organisation – or ensure that a revitalised PRA has sufficient funds and the capability to put pre-retirement training on an effective basis.

The votes held by existing pensioners and those within five years of retirement exceed 16,000,000. Anything is possible!

Bibliography

Approach to Retirement Kit, Pre-Retirement Association.

Executive Ease and Disease, Dr Beric Wright, Pan Books, 1977. 90p.

Looking Ahead, A Guide to Retirement, Fred Kemp and Bernard Buttle, Continua Publications Ltd, 1977. £1.00, or £1.20 post paid from the Pre-Retirement Association.

Money and Your Retirement, Edward Eves, Pre-Retirement Association, 1978. £1.25.

Retirement Move — Longer than a Holiday, leaflet listing points to consider when moving house. 20p post paid from the Pre-Retirement Association.

'Tax Guide', *Daily Mail,* available from all bookshops. 50p.

Working for Free, Sheila Moore, Pan Books, 1977.

Working for Yourself, The *Daily Telegraph* Guide to Self-Employment, Godfrey Golzen, Kogan Page, (revised edition 1978).
(Includes an appendix on retirement and the self-employed person).

Your Rights, Age Concern.

Please note that the first five publications mentioned are available direct from: The Pre-Retirement Association, 19 Undine Street, Tooting, London SW17 8PP. (Tel 01-767 3225)

Useful Addresses

Abbeyfield Society
35A High Street
Potters Bar
Hertfordshire EN6 5DL
Tel 77 43371

National organisation with affiliated local
bodies catering for elderly people to live in
family homes.

Age Concern
60 Pitcairn Road
Mitcham
Surrey
Tel 01-640 5431

Publishes *Your Rights* for pensioners.
Over 1,000 local groups offer welfare
services for the retired.

Anchor Housing Association
Oxenford House
13-15 Magdalen Street
Oxford OX1 3BP
Tel 0865 22261

Back Pain Association
Grundy House
Teddington TW11 8TD
Tel 01-977 1171

Promotes and finances research into the
causes, cures and prevention of back pain.
Publishes *You and Your Back* in paperback
form.

British Diabetic Association
10 Queen Anne Street
London W1M 0BD
Tel 01-323 1531

General guidance on diet, insulin, and
medical equipment but does not give
individual advice.

British Life Assurance Trust
    for Health Education
BLAT Centre for Health
    and Medical Education
BMA House
Tavistock Square
London WC1H 9JP
Tel 01-385 7976

Promotes innovation in health and medical
education. Has produced multi-media
audio-visual packages dealing with
retirement education.

British Red Cross Society
9 Grosvenor Crescent
London SW1X 7EJ
Tel 01-235 5454

Provides many community services
including transport for the sick.

British Rheumatism and
   Arthritis Association
6 Grosvenor Crescent
London SW1X 7EH
Tel 01-235 0902

Runs a welfare service, a residential home
for the badly crippled, holidays; gives
information on aids, and publishes a
Review quarterly.

British Standards Institution
Consumer Affairs Department
2 Park Street
London W1A 2BS
Tel 01-629 9000

Tests products to ensure they meet with
accepted standards

BUPA Medical Centre
Battle Bridge House
300 Gray's Inn Road
London WC1
Tel 01-278 8931

BUPA is an insurance company covering
people against costs of private medical care.
The BUPA Medical Centre is a registered
charity for promoting health and the
prevention of disease (see chapter 5).

Buretire

see Employment Fellowship

The Chest, Heart and Stroke
   Association
Tavistock House North
Tavistock Square
London WC1H 9JE
Tel 01-387 3012

Gives advice on individual problems and
produces leaflets and general publications.

Choice Magazine
Bedford Chambers
Covent Garden
London WC2E 8HA
Tel 01-836 8772

The only magazine for retirement planning.

Church Army Housing Ltd
Welford House
Shirland Road
London W9
Tel 01-289 2241

Consumers' Association
14 Buckingham Street
London WC2N 6DS
Tel 01-839 1222

Useful information on the value of everyday
issues. Publishes *Which* magazine and
booklets on a wide range of subjects.

Department of Health and
   Social Security (DHSS)
Information Division Leaflets Unit
Block 4, Government Buildings
Honeypot Lane
Stanmore
Middlesex HA7 1AY
Tel 01-952 2311

Disabled Living Foundation
346 Kensington High Street
London W14
Tel 01-602 2491

Helps with enquiries on suitable aids for
particular disabilities. Exhibition of aids can
be viewed by appointment only.

Employment Fellowship
Drayton House
Gordon Street
London WC1H 0BE
Tel 01-387 1828

Concerned with various schemes including: work centres for the elderly, retirement industries centre, and Buretire (employment bureau for the retired).

Friends of the Earth
9 Poland Street
London W1V 3DG
Tel 01-437 6121

The Health Education Council
78 New Oxford Street
London WC1A 1AH
Tel 01-637 1881

Issues leaflets on subjects including: Heating in the home, Home safety, Medicines, Care of the Elderly, and Look after yourself.

Help the Aged
32 Dover Street
London W1A 2AP
Tel 01-499 0972

Promotes sheltered housing, day centres and facilities for the elderly. Publishes *Yours* newspaper.

The Housing Corporation
149 Tottenham Court Road
London W1P 0BN
Tel 01-387 9466

Gives information on housing associations in all localities.

The Law Society
113 Chancery Lane
London WC2A 1PL
Tel 01-242 1222

Provides a leaflet on will-making and addresses of local solicitors.

The Life Offices' Association
Aldermary House
Queen Street
London EC4N 1TP
Tel 01-236 5117

Can supply details of companies offering mortgage annuity schemes (see chapter 8).

London Council of Social Service
(Volunteers Advisory Service)
68 Chalton Street
London NW1 1JR
Tel 01-388 0241

National Council for the Single
    Woman and her Dependants
29 Chilworth Mews
London W2 3RG
Tel 01-262 1451

National Council of Social Service
Community Works Division
26 Bedford Square
London WC1B 3HU
Tel 01-636 4066

Can supply addresses of volunteer bureaux, Councils for voluntary service, Federations of community associations and rural community councils in Britain.

National Federation of Housing
    Societies
30-32 Southampton Street
Strand
London WC2E 7HE
Tel 01-240 2771

Gives information on housing associations throughout the UK.

191

National Institute of Adult
    Education
De Montfort House
19B De Montfort Street
Leicester LE1 7GH
Tel 0533 538977

Advisory and consultative body reflecting nationally the interests of organisations, institutions and individuals concerned in the provision of adult education. Provides information and periodicals, including calendar of residential short courses.

Office of Fair Trading
Field House
Breams Buildings
London EC4
Tel 01-242 2858

Collates information on all consumer problems and trading matters.

The Open University
Information Services Department
Walton Hall
Milton Keynes MK7 6AA

Part-time Careers Ltd
10 Golden Square
London W1
Tel 01-437 3103

Can assist with finding long-term or part-time office work.

People's Dispensary for Sick
    Animals
Head Office
PDSA House
South Street
Dorking
Tel 0306 81691

PDSA animal treatment centres in most large towns provide free treatment for sick and injured animals if owners cannot afford private veterinary fees.

Pre-Retirement Association
    of Great Britain and
    Northern Ireland
19 Undine Street
Tooting
London SW17 8PP
Tel 01-767 3225

The National Association dealing with preparation for retirement. Distributes retirement kits and current retirement publications.

Retirement Homes Association Ltd
Southdowns
South Darenth
Dartford
Kent DA14 9LG
Tel 0322 864279

Operates specially designed retirement communities (see chapter 9 for details).

Royal Association for Disability
    and Rehabilitation
25 Mortimer Street
London W1N 8AB
Tel 01-637 5400

Information centre concerned with aids, welfare, mobility, insurance, holidays and housing for physically handicapped people.

The Royal British Legion Housing
    Association
35 Jackson Court
Hazlemere
High Wycombe
Buckinghamshire HP15 7TX
Tel 049481 3771

Saga Holidays Ltd
119 Sandgate Road
Folkestone
Kent CT20 2BN
Tel 0303 57300

Holiday specialists for senior citizens.

Seymour, Pierce & Co
10 Old Jewry
London EC2R 8EA
Tel 01-628 4981

Publishes lists of concessionary
discounts available to shareholders in
UK companies.

Success After Sixty
(Office Employment Ltd)
14 Great Castle Street
London W1
Tel 01-580 8932

Can assist with finding office jobs for
retired people. Also has branches in
Croydon, Slough and Manchester.

Volunteer Centre
29 Lower Kings Road
Berkhamsted
Hertfordshire HP4 2AB
Tel 04427 73311

Index

Research, 149
Responsibility for training, 145
Retirement homes, 137-42
Retirement Homes Association, 138-42
Retirement issue, National Savings, 55
Retirement kits, 162
Retirement migration, 114
Rheumatism, 80
Role-playing, 38-9
Role, seeking new, 38-40
Routine, 27
Royal Institution of Chartered Surveyors, The, 120, 122

Safety in the home, 130-1
Saga Holidays, 50
Save as you earn (SAYE), 54
Schedule A, 48
Schedule B, 49
Security in the home, 133-4
Seeking advice, 40
Self-employed, 58-9
Service to community, 106
Sexual activity, 68
Seymour Pierce and Co, 57-8
Shakespeare, 38, 40, 99
Shares with perks, 57-8
Sheltered housing, 142-3
Sheltered workshops, 103
Single people, 35-6
Sleep, 67
Smoking, 67
Social contacts, 25
South Africa, 180
Spain, 181
State Retirement Pension, 41-4, 57, 109-10, 134
Status, 24, 39
Stockbrokers, 53
Stress, 64-5
Supplementary Pension, 56-7
Surveys, see House surveys
Switzerland, 181-2
Sykes, Kay, 102

Teeth, 81
Tenancies, 123
Tenants (non-Council House), 130
Trade unions, 153-4
Training Opportunities Scheme (TOPS), 103, 153
Training Services Division, 153
Travel costs, 41, 46, 50, 119
Trustee Savings Bank, 52

Unemployment Benefit Office, 108
United Nations Office, Division of Social Affairs, 21
Unit Trusts, 53
Universities, 94, 160
Unmarried women, 35-6
USA, 172, 182-3, 185-6

Voluntary help organisers, 107
Voluntary services, 154-8
Voluntary work, 106
Volunteers Advisory Service, 106

Watkin Williams, G, 106
Weight, 68-70
W H Smith seminar, 169
Wills, see Making a will
Women's Royal Voluntary Service, 156-7
'Workaholics', 23, 100
Workers' Educational Association, 159, 161
Workshops for the elderly, 105
World Health Organisation, 63, 64

Years Still Unexplored, The, 21